Seven Shades of J

SEVEN SHADES OF J

Accounts of
longing, lust and bipolar

Recalled by Jean Riley
and written by L. Halliwell

Copyright © 2018 Jean Riley and L. Halliwell

The moral right of the author has been asserted.

Apart from any fair dealing for the purposes of research or private study, or criticism or review, as permitted under the Copyright, Designs and Patents Act 1988, this publication may only be reproduced, stored or transmitted, in any form or by any means, with the prior permission in writing of the publishers, or in the case of reprographic reproduction in accordance with the terms of licences issued by the Copyright Licensing Agency. Enquiries concerning reproduction outside those terms should be sent to the publishers.

Matador
9 Priory Business Park,
Wistow Road, Kibworth Beauchamp,
Leicestershire. LE8 0RX
Tel: 0116 279 2299
Email: books@troubador.co.uk
Web: www.troubador.co.uk/matador
Twitter: @matadorbooks

ISBN 978 1789014 235

British Library Cataloguing in Publication Data.
A catalogue record for this book is available from the British Library.

Printed and bound in Great Britain by 4edge Limited
Typeset in 11pt Minion Pro by Troubador Publishing Ltd, Leicester, UK

Matador is an imprint of Troubador Publishing Ltd

*To Rob and Caroline
for their love and forbearance.*

Contents

In my own words...
- ix -

1 ~ *Just a Dead Flame's Shade*
- 1 -

2 ~ *A New Life and a Deadly Shade*
- 19 -

3 ~ *In the Shade of Gun Smoke and Mops*
- 40 -

4 ~ *In the Shade of the Millennium*
- 54 -

5 ~ *In the Shade of the Palace*
- 70 -

6 ~ *Shades within a Mirage*
- 88 -

7 ~ *A Shade of Blood Red*
- 99 -

Humanity... a suitable case for treatment!
- 111 -

In my own words...

I had always been considered a 'highly strung' child and an adult given to strong emotion, but no one ever told me I was mentally ill. So, for me, it was amidst heartbreak and through a husband's disloyalty that bipolar was born.

The narratives that follow are based on my personal experience of Bipolar Affective Disorder, which I was first diagnosed with in 1985 after the catastrophic effect of my divorce from my first husband and the father of my son and daughter. He had always been a 'flirt', but it was only after my divorce that the true extent of his infidelities became known to me, involving those I thought of as friends. I'm sure I'm not the only woman who has endured an unhappy, sexless marriage. However, the consequences affected the course of my life and, at times, my safety.

Like many sufferers I was prescribed Haloperidol, which seemed to take away what I would describe as my zest for life. Being who I am, I made a decision not to take the medication prescribed, ergo any emotional upset meant my mood elevated beyond belief, and certainly beyond what I could manage. It was only after encounters of the sexual kind in Tunisia that I began to accept the need for me to take medication regularly, even if I felt no need to do so.

A meeting with a female psychiatrist, one with a willingness to discuss and review my needs, meant that I began to take Resperidone and Carbamazepine. We both settled on a dosage which kept me in equilibrium, and enabled me to have a sense of self. The result was quite remarkable, dare I say, miraculous.

I have had two voluntary admissions to psychiatric hospitals and have been sectioned under the Mental Health Act four times, in the Midlands, in London, and even in Norway! I take medication daily now, always at night because of the soporific effects. I avoid loud music and shy away from emotional situations, if at all possible, because I know these can have a marked effect on me at any time. This self-management, along with my regular consultations with a psychiatrist, has led me to believe that major turmoil is in the past.

I have spent money unwisely. I have given away valuable jewellery, and have some broken and strained relationships with friends and family members, but I enjoy a deal of stability. I earnestly wish that others with the same condition do so too. I am fortunate to have the support of a circle of female friends, Pam and Ria especially. I have stretched their patience to the limit. Pam has suffered my endless phone calls at all times of day and night with not a word of admonishment. Their kindness and forbearance has been truly heroic.

Without my dear Lesley, my story would not have been written. She has been a blessing and I thank the Lord for our chance meeting on a visit to Rome, Easter 2006. Magical! When I spoke of my journey with bipolar over many years, I told her that the condition had not made me into a victim, and that I must not be painted as such. In fact, I did make it clear that she should recount all candidly with humour and verve.

Say what you will, bipolar is here to stay in my life. In many ways, I am glad, because it makes me feel that life is utterly marvellous. Indeed, I still feel that I was at my most creative zenith during an episode, but maybe some would disagree with me. I need to have balance in my life, but I must confess I enjoy the days more when my mood is rather more buoyant than the average. Don't we all need a little more than the hum-drum? Still, I feel that the worst thing would be for my life to be boring.

Do enjoy sharing these, my life's experiences and the shades in between which I guess will trouble, enthral and delight you!

1 Just a Dead Flame's Shade

"Look at it burn," Jean said to herself.

Television was her window to the world and the easiest distraction from her marriage, which had become a source of daily unease. Jean watched the news and films the most. One caught her eye, and she soon realised that everything she saw was somehow connected with fire. She watched York Minster burn for the whole world to see, and Richy, her latest interesting man, reminded her of 'Old Nick' himself, smouldering in his cigarette smoke and alcoholic fug. Things were beginning to become jumbled in together. A fire was kindling inside Jean's soul; Richy was becoming her obsession.

She had been thinking a lot lately. She decided that her marriage was old hat. Raif was off and about somewhere with some other female or two. He had become the classic absent husband and father. There was also the matter of her own parents; they were back on the scene, worried and checking on her. They came into view and receded again in Jean's thinking. She fancied that she had pursued them to Stamford Hall, but she could have imagined that.

Things real and not quite so real constantly came and went. One thing she was sure about was that she must do something. And whatever the Lord had ordained, she knew she must do it properly. She had fire in her belly for change, and come it would...

* * *

The television continued to show images of the smouldering Minster. Memories intruded. It made Jean nostalgic, thinking of visits there in her past. She had time on her hands, and thoughts and memories raced one on to the other. She remembered her younger days, when she'd been taught that there is always a way to do things properly. Jean had been brought up in the proper manner; her mother had run her highly prestigious nursing home with calm efficiency in the proper manner. Her Home for Older Ladies and Gents was at pains to play down prostate troubles, dementing tendencies and bowel habits. No dementia or Alzheimer's there, just the wealthy elite of Bournemouth. Sherry was served at eleven sharp on Sundays, and all of the residents were well-connected. It was a major selling point, especially for relatives in denial. Her husband was not so sure, but no matter. Her mother's business was successful without a doubt. In business, if something was worth doing, it was worth doing well.

Ditto life.

Ditto suicide.

Jean was not happy. The thought of her own suicide grew ever stronger. She could not steal away from the insistent voice that she must die, and soon. It seemed utterly logical that this must be the next step. And if you were going to end it all, you had to do it with dignity if you were going to do it at all. Of that Jean was sure.

Thoughts of suicide were becoming her pastime. The Americans called it 'closure'. For Jean, it must be a final way out. With a marriage in the doldrums and boredom – something had to be done.

She had inherited her mother's effervescent commitment to making the ordinary quite exceptional. It was only proper, and you may as well make the whole thing as pleasurable as possible. Suicide, that is. Do it and do it well. Why sell yourself short when you didn't need to? Jean knew her marriage must end and maybe herself with it. In her mind, suicide seemed to be a must. It seemed the right thing to do – the show-stopper type suicide, that is – the classic last act that would be singled out by onlookers. Especially as your suicide would be your finale; you had to bear in mind that there would be no curtain call. So, you had to make sure it was the act that couldn't be followed. The thing your public remembered.

"I must look my best," Jean determined. She knew she must be camera-ready before she digested the pills along with the spirit of her choice. There was planning to be done. It would be, perhaps, the most defining moment of her life which she alone would orchestrate. Her manner of slipping off the mortal coil would always be remembered as quite marvellous, she was sure of that. She wondered what reaction Raif would have. After all, they were still married, and he was the father of her children even though he was absent.

The delight of being in charge of one's life and death stirred her spirits. It was a good feeling to be in control. Jean imagined the newspaper headlines, and her only regret was that she would not have a hand in writing them. No interviews would be given by her. What a wasted opportunity. The suicide would prevent her verbalising meaningful, poignant statements about her philosophy of life, love, death, beauty regime and fashion sense. No way round it, but it was a regret. She would have liked to have held the moment and made the six o'clock local news at the very least.

The day came.

Alone, with her mind made up, Jean shut the cycle shop early. Richy, her new, special male friend, had not called at the shop that day. It was a disappointment. He said he would. Jean felt the cold shoulder. He may have taken her mind away from her death wish, but he did not come. She locked up the shop methodically and left for home. You can't be too careful, opportunist thieves were everywhere these days.

She could not really remember getting back to the house. Raif was not there, of course. Everything seemed very dark. She was alone. It was time to prepare for a good ending.

She lit the fire. She liked a log fire and insisted on a clean grate. That night its flames crackled with tragic, glassy-eyed, romantic irony – nothing less would be acceptable. Hedda Gabler could not have made a better effort.

Jean enjoyed the scene that she had chosen. She cradled it. It was her conception. Her death set. She arranged the sofa and its silky cushions; it was quilted with coffin-hugging promise. Satisfied, Jean felt she was in charge. This act would prove that she had the upper hand in overcoming the death of her marriage to Raif, which had not been the Hollywood idyll, despite their golden couple reputation.

She lay back and thought about her husband to be in 1963. When she had first set eyes on Raif he was handsome to a turn, though she told him that she couldn't see what all the fuss was about. Secretly, she triumphed in his charisma, his image, his talk about cars and gadding. She was the girl who wore the pink velour hat, odd and splendid. Their meeting in the espresso bar was a key scene showing at Cannes in her mind's eye. It was Julie Christie and Captain Troy – all meant to be, with just the right blend of devil-may-care and no-hope attraction.

All gone.

There was no need for speech or explanation. She would not leave a note. There was no need to verbalise the void, the burn out. There would be no point. Tonight, there would be no lovers looking into the fire's flames or remembering the burn of love Cartland-style. No shared flame reflected between lovers' eyes. Tonight there was only one glass. A bottle unshared.

The surroundings said it all. It was passion and failure, spent dreams and the mortgage unpaid. Tonight Jean lived the hopelessness of Anna Karenina. Holst's Planets with undertones of Elton John bolstered her senses, speaking to her and finalising the moment.

They, her public, would find her recumbent, well-dressed, stylish as ever, and they would all be overcome with the spectacle of it all. Her hair was a good colour at present with a smart cut to suit. They would all look at her and comment that death had not pinched away her looks. She imagined the funeral; they would all say that she had so much to live for. Her death would dictate the plans for the living. Her husband and lovers would be reunited. They would embrace. Someone would throw a party in her memory, she was sure. The men in her life would assume a brotherhood of understanding, and Jean's final action would be the authoress of this union. There could be nothing better, nothing grander.

Some things are worth dying for.

* * *

Later. Later. She did not know how long later. Time had passed. The pills had not worked. In hospital, they had pumped out her stomach. She told them she was fine and they sent her home to be with family and friends.

Jean did not know how much time had passed but she always seemed to be home alone, the same thoughts returning. It was all connected, with York Minster somewhere along the line. Yes, she had survived her suicide attempt, caught in the nick of time, but Jean's soul could not rest. Her mission for something grand in life or death pressed in on her senses. The sight of the fire on the news reels roused her again. Thoughts raced, Jean pictured the scene with herself in it; arching, spitting flames swallowed up the dark in magical orange and red stains, dancing and obliterating the blackness. The voices spoke to her, the flaming image returned and returned again, chasing into her thoughts without warning. It was a rousing challenge which she could not exorcise.

Then, she returned to the voices in the present, concerned and drilling in on her thinking causing the Minster to retreat for the time being. She thought of Raif's words the morning after the night she had swallowed the pills. He had called her 'a bloody mess'. Hardly tender loving care. Never in her whole life could she ever be described thus! She loathed his insensitivity, but she marginalised it because there were more important things to think about. She dwelt instead on the fire she'd lit that night – the crackling log flames licking the grate.

Another flame still burned. She had a penchant for Richy. He was an ongoing thought. One day he would be hers, she knew, but she put him on hold. Her last image of him slumped behind an overflowing ashtray, cigarette end burning like an orange button, his smile wry and relaxed and intriguing, woolly in his jumper. He had a certain lure. She would have her tryst with him. It was only a matter of time. He would succumb as soon as she could wangle her complete freedom from her marriage.

* * *

"Jean, Jean! Stop day-dreaming." It was the voice of her mother. She was staying with Jean to make sure she didn't do anything reckless again. Her mother wanted her to be stable.

"We can all dream," Jean said in a huff.

"Jean we need to talk," her mother said, ignoring her daughter's cheek. "You have to start taking the tablets that the experts say you must. We don't want a repeat performance of the other night. Another stomach pumping episode would kill you!"

Jean gathered herself into the present. Her mother was cramping her style. She spoke authoritatively, peering at her mother. "Don't be ridiculous – I've never felt more alive in my whole life."

She saw she was looking back at her with annoying concern and continued, irritated. "You've got it all wrong. I don't need tablets. Everything is absolutely bloody marvellous! I am over the blip."

She eyed her mother and sensed that there must be some counter conspiracy afoot.

Her son cajoled. "Come on Mum, time for bed. You need a good rest. You've only just come out of the Infirmary. We don't want you back there again, do we?"

Jean was having none of it. She spoke with ceremony. "The stomach is pumped. The wrongs are righted. Psychiatrists were humoured. The doctor has had his way. All's well that ends well." She smiled pertly.

Conversation over.

After a suitable time-lapse Jean made her way to the window and twitched the curtains wider open eager to view the outside world. She wanted to escape to pilot her new acquisitions. Jean had been spending money on sports cars. Lots of money. It was the only way to win back some of the exhilaration she longed for.

She looked outside. No sign of the cars she had ordered. Bugger.

Then she recalled that her mother had mentioned that she would be sending them all back to the showroom. Jean liked a good car, sleek and fast just like her men.

"No good looking for those sports cars. They aren't there love. The garage took them back when I explained you'd had a bad turn," her mother said firmly.

It was a bit of a blow as Jean had been looking forward to launching the new fleet with son and daughter as driver two and three. They had accused her of being OTT. The dream was not to become a reality after all. More disappointment. When were people going to actually start tasting life's juices like she did?

With dreary acceptance, Jean remembered that she had agreed to bear the wet blanket that her mother had applied to her latest phase. This was irking as, in past times, Jean remembered that her mother had been ready to encourage the grand happenings, indeed she had instigated one or two herself when Jean had been younger.

Today, there was no daredevil ally she could inspire to collude with, nevertheless a mission defined itself in Jean's mind. Her secret thoughts were fanning her passion into flame. She could not deny the call. She was accustomed to going it alone if she had to. As the Lord had tested Job, so she too would expect to be tested and rise to the occasion against the odds. Appearances could be very deceptive, Jean knew that. She must push forward. A lot rested on her. The world would be a poorer place if she gave into those around her who were misguided and lacked courage. There was world peace to secure. There was sex to be had. There was money to be spent.

Jean's awareness was electric. Every detail was a palpable hit to every nerve ending. She was alive and kicking and there was so much to do. So many things to achieve. So many thoughts to action and put to bed. There was no time to lose, and the thought of tablets designed to blunt her energy and visionary surges was totally ludicrous.

And there was the Minster to consider. The image of its burning grandeur kept on surfacing, the vision of its messages written in those hallowed flames formed and reformed in her mind as she moved and spoke. Richy appeared superimposed in front of the Minster. He was smiling a wicked smile too and lit a cigarette, another glint in her mind's eye. The Minster's flames leapt higher and higher. Jean felt them in her abdomen, on her back and throat. They gathered momentum in one glorious crackling storm of light and fire. It was a sign she needed to heed. It was God's voice.

She knew she must decipher the flames' movements, translate them into the written word, gird her loins and take the plunge. She knew that the Minster's destruction was the workings of the Creator, His sign to her. He was obviously aggrieved. And no wonder, just look at the world; misguided and Godless humanity snivelled around in the charred dregs of bad politicians' rhetoric, northerners on the rampage and single mothers in Council houses. There were also rumblings of war with religious unrest beating its wings in the Middle East souring the Lord's plan. Something had to give.

The world needed the Messiah more than ever to secure world peace, not to mention common sense. She must heed the call. "I'm coming," Jean said aloud. It was time for her to take up the Eternal Laurel. Peace would bring an end to the deaths. She knew she must act soon. She could either ignore or destroy the obstacles. The doubters, the unimaginative dullards and the NHS pill pushers must be kicked into touch.

She sat back and closed her eyes knowing that the onlookers would be pleased with her seemingly compliant. She could handle her family, but meanwhile, Jean spied the Messiah. Her vision of him was real enough to touch. He strode the horizon against a flame swirled backdrop.

Curiously, Jean noted that he appeared to have her face. "Tis me," she whispered with a fervent gaze.

* * *

She hated mornings at the best of times. This morning was worse than usual because today she must ward off the machinations of the Mental Health Act and her mother yet again. Her mother was keen for Jean to spend time in a Mental Health Unit with the experts on hand.

"Get it into your heads," Jean said forcibly. "I am not going to any hospital, psychiatric or otherwise. I've had it up to here with all of you. I do not need a hospital bed or pills or any form of electric shock. Got it?" She eye-balled her mother and the doctor she had drafted in to make Jean's removal to a 'place of safety' official.

"The Towers is a very nice hospital. The grounds are lovely and the patients make things and do the garden. I've seen them over the fence."

"Really?" Jean said totally disinterested. The idea of basket weaving and standing in a potting shed did not set her imagination on fire, though the vision of the Minster's fire still flickered amidst the urgings and pleadings she must endure.

"They know what they're doing, and you'll be sorted out in no time at all, Jean. ECT is the new wonder drug, but without the drug. It cleans your brain up. Isn't science wonderful?"

Jean elected to be mute. Sometimes it was the only way.

"See sense," her mother coaxed her. "You can't go on running around, Jean. We can't run the risk of another stomach pumping, can we? We don't know what you're going to do next. The neighbours keep giving us funny looks as well, so it's for the best Jean." Mid-sentence she looked towards the doctor and adopted a hushed tone in order to put him in the picture. "She was a wilful child, you know. You'll have to be firm with her otherwise she'll run us all ragged."

Doctor Williams, devoid of bed-side manner took the cue and assumed an air of gravity. "You're going to hospital now, young lady. No ifs or buts."

Jean Riley

Tired and more than a little bored, Jean decided it would be better to accept the offer of a hospital stay, and the attention of a psychiatrist rather than be forced to regress into her adolescent self with her mother in control.

With a defiant shrug Jean adjusted her outfit knowing that she cut a thin and interesting figure. With a toss of her head and in a Broadway drawl she told them both to, "Bring it on!"

* * *

Time came and went. Jean was the model patient and once her treatment was completed, she was discharged. It said 'Discharged – relieved' on the chitty they had given her at the hospital on the way out. They told her to see her GP and he would monitor her mental wellbeing. So be it.

Back home again Jean sat still, thinking. She was not subdued for long. The latest hospital admission has slowed her in her tracks, but the calling was still there. The mission must be fulfilled. She began to see the embers of York Minster soaked with rain, the fire extinguished. However, the electro-convulsive treatments had not erased the decadent lure of Richy.

"I want him," Jean declared aloud. That spark was alive. She was not done with sex. Her marriage was over and husband gone, but not sexual creature she was and would always be. She must be satisfied. She would make an opening when the time was right and to hell with the consequences.

She was still Raif's wife in name, though she had thrown him out of the marital home because of his latest female interest. Raif had been sheepish because he'd been up to something with another 'special' female. You never knew. That was the problem. Jean never knew, and this had been the source of unrest over the years.

However, a surprise visit from Raif's sister and family became a focus. They were curious about the impact of the ECT on Jean. She would prove that she could play her 'indoors' as well as any other role she chose; she could be the ideal hostess at the drop of a hat.

"I need to buy champagne for tonight. Nothing less. I'm not skimping. I'm home. I survived the Towers. I think we should celebrate."

Jean moved quickly around the house. She was focussed on catering for Raif's sister and children. It would all be marvellous. Jean would give them a night to remember. She would make them see that she was made of strong stuff. She would show she was a good wife, despite her cad of a husband. She may have had seven treatments of ECT guinea-pig style, but she would show them all that her spirit would never be quenched. Convulsed and shocked she had been; defeated she was not. Tonight, she would bust another myth they had spun about her natural creativity which they, her family and doctors, in their half-baked view of the world, called mental illness.

"I'm off to shop. Don't worry – the lunatic will return armed with smoked salmon and champagne," she told her mother, who remained concerned. She had seen the twinkle in Jean's eye before. Doubtless there would be something new around the corner. What that might be was, as yet, another mystery. She watched Jean leave with her shopping bag after elaborate goodbyes. Everything was so normal, on the surface. It was Jean's first outing from the house alone since her treatment in the hospital. She was going shopping just like millions of other women and yet there was nothing ordinary about Jean.

She stepped into the fresh air and began to live her 'me time'. She could still blaze a trail. It would take more than a few electrodes to snuff her candle.

* * *

In time, Jean's 'me time' turned its attention to Richy. He wasn't exactly a substitute for Raif, but he was a man. She needed her 'Old Nick' to emerge from the embers of York Minster in her mind's eye. She would pay Richy a visit. She was a desirable woman, after all.

She knocked on his door and waited. It was a strange time for a visitor to call. Richy sidled into his hallway, a little worse for wear, and opened his front door.

"Hello Richy. I've come to finish that crossword we started." Jean stood in the doorway, bright-eyed, tongue on her rose budlips. "I miss your little visits. Have you missed me?"

He smiled, a bit bleary, and edged backwards as Jean entered his house and the fug of the living room. "I thought they'd locked you up," he said retrieving his cigarette from a burgeoning ash tray. He hollowed his cheeks and stifled a cough. Jean noticed that he was wearing odd socks, but his thighs looked ready and inviting.

"It's all in the past. I gave in. I've had the new treatment, seven of the buggers and I have a clean bill of health. Voila! What you see is what you get… and do you like what you see?"

Jean was vivacious. She had escaped the humdrum and tonight she was the Bohemian she had always wanted to be. Richy brought it out of her. He was a man.

"I've missed you, Richy," she said. "I loved it when you used to visit the shop. A lot seems to have happened since we got together then." She felt herself in the sway of the laissez-faire that he exuded. She seated herself next to him crossing her legs, poised and expectant.

"I've had champagne and smoked salmon and did the family thing tonight, but I'm here now. For you, dearest. Come here." She gripped his jumper tight, pulling him near to her mouth.

"Yes," Richy said not totally at ease, swaying a little, his jumper redolent with nicotine.

"I've been thinking about you a lot. You see we have a lot in common, don't we Richy? There are those chats in the bike shop – you keep coming back – and there are the crosswords. Two heads are better than one! And tarot cards you gave me. I've been looking into the future. It sort of makes sense us being together." Jean's gaze was magnetic. "And you hold a bit of a torch for me, don't you?"

"Torch?"

"Yes. Torch. 'Come on, light my fire' and all that… who sang that song? Anyway, speaking of torches, wasn't it awful about York Minster?" Jean's vision changed. It was all so meaningful the way snapshots returned and retreated when you least expected it. She tried to remember the number of times she had pictured fires and flames in the last month. Now, as she relaxed, myriad spits of fire made patterns in her mind's eye. Jean pressed her head on to Richy's shoulder. To her delight he had muscles under his checked shirt. "Um, nice," she said.

Richy lit another cigarette and held his lighter flame open. "Did you want one, Jean? Might calm things a bit."

"Yes, I will." She rolled the tube between her fingers in a suggestive way, and pulled down Richy's hand so that the naked flame lit the cigarette between her pursed lips. It could have been a scene from Casablanca. She drew on it still fixing Richy with her gaze. "Well?" she said.

Richy sat back, swallowed up into the settee. It sagged and was a bit unkempt, but it fulfilled its purpose.

"Well," he said nervously. "You do realise that they'll lock you up again if you don't take the medication."

Glib and rebellious and just a little sultry, Jean was determined to be churlish. She recalled a film she had seen. Richy was her Jack Nicholson – Old Nick in his sagging dressing gown sozzled with whiskey. Despite his smoker's cough, for Jean, he was irresistible in his maleness.

"No way. The fires of hell will have to freeze over first," she said, taunting and flirtatious. She would have her Richy tonight, she thought, eyeing his stubble.

She proffered a kiss. Richy faced her and then stubbed out his cigarette. He did not speak, but Jean sensed that he was bracing himself. This was a promising sign, Jean thought. She clutched his fly area and he edged forward and then back. He said nothing, but Jean detected a grimace. She rolled her eyes in readiness then dug in a little deeper. Her hand would do its magic. She was not one for giving in. Soon the serpent would stir. Surely. She knew it would take time, bathed in the effects of the whiskey as it was, but Jean could be a patient woman when she had to be. Helping things along, she inserted her hand deeper and the reptile's pink head emerged, ever so slightly at first. She looked at it, then puckered up. It was the only way.

"Don't be shy," Jean said in her tigress voice. She squeezed hard. Richy closed his eyes and adjusted his buttocks to accommodate Jean's grip. She coaxed the beast. She released, reddened and dove again. He floundered. The image of the Minster flashed ahead of her. She dove again, and the tongues of fire leapt even higher.

2 A New Life and a Deadly Shade

"Fabulous," Jean said loudly above the television.

The volume in Jean's bedroom was switched up high. It was good to have the senses awakened at full pelt. The Royal Variety Performance was hitting the spot; the lights, the gowns, and the dickies and cummerbunds were visually magnificent. Nearly everything bore a shimmer no matter where Jean set her gaze. The Royal Variety Performance had always been a feast for her soul, so much so that everything started to become extremely vivid, layered with meanings and opportunities. Real life was beginning to take hold again.

And Jean had ditched the medication.

It had been the winter of her discontent; she had been in the wilderness for more than forty days, as was the Lord. Now, somehow her ideas had the promise of bespangled moments. Jean was in need of a playmate and the TV glitterati summoned her to life anew this evening. The message could not have been louder or clearer.

She watched the line-up after the show. Her Majesty, magnetic as ever spoke to nearly every performer. Her royal mouth moved in her well-bred habit. Jean felt very much at one with her monarch. She was confident that the Queen would be making every second special for these showbiz types such as they were – good, bad, and indifferent.

Speaking of indifferent, the image of 'the barmaid' who was now living in rented accommodation with the father of her children sprang into Jean's mind.

"Bloody wasp-belted floozy," Jean said aloud, hardly moving her lips. She had had her belly full of dealing with the 'other woman', and a husband who liked to forage. Her own affair with Peter Cramp was a fact. True. But Peter Cramp was history, even though she did think back to those wonderful afternoon romps from time to time. The Peter caper was something she needed to do – a bit of 'me' time – but for her husband, women had always been a way of life. And what a life it had turned out to be.

For a second, the terrible past crept back into her memory again. They had married young. Jean remembered the tears in Raif's eyes when all started to go awry. She willed the image to diminish, but it lingered a little. Jean saw herself. She was playing the piano in her own concerto-styled way that spoke to his inner man, to the best of him. They had all said that she was ill, but for her, that 'awful' time was her most creative period. She was not ill; merely giving vent to the genius within. It was hard to understand or see it as others did.

She remembered back to that moment when words were not enough to tell her anguish, but her piano playing could. She remembered how she had touched the keys with tender, delicate meaning – the hurt rising in aggression through the tone of how she played. It was her mouthpiece, beautiful and disarming for Raif, but it had not been enough for him or for herself.

The love-tie that bound them from youth must be severed. He was gone.

The memory faded out. Jean came back to herself with a shake, like when somebody walks over your grave. She would have liked to give Raif hell again right now, both barrels. Had he taken leave of his senses? The fool. What had possessed him to desire a woman who thought current affairs was a type of pastry? What on Earth did he see in a woman who wore a wasp belt? Jean had it for a fact that certain local men knew that 'the barmaid' was not a natural blonde.

Raif had gone to concerts and read the quality press for heaven's sake. He could do the Times Crossword. Jean saw to it that he was erudite, and he was. You either had it or you didn't – and she and Raif had it. Class that is. And there he was now shacked up with every man's favourite barmaid.

It really was enough to turn you to drink.

Jean switched her thinking quickly. There were more important things in the present to consider. It was Boxing

Day and she was going out. Going out as a single woman. It was exciting. She must be sophisticated, not too keen, and have an air of wealth and independence. Above all, she must be desirable. Jean looked at herself in the mirror sideways on, and then a full frontal. A couple of her fingers were crusted with her mother's diamonds. She truly would be lighting up the room tonight.

She was very glad that her neighbour, Ria, had invited her to her Boxing Day party. It was a big house just across the A6 with a big entrance, and Jean was confident that her vivacious self, her outfit and the diamonds would fit it easily. She knew that everyone present would be asking who she was. It would be like the old days when Jean daredevilled herself into whatever and whoever she chose.

Jean heard her mother approaching on the stairs. "You look lovely Jean," her mother said taking a long look at her daughter. She must make a fuss over Jean by way of relieving a mother's anxiety. "My rings go a treat. You still have a certain something, don't you? Christmas and diamonds go together, don't they? You need a night out, Jean. We hope you have a good time, but be careful."

"Yes," Jean sighed.

"Not too much to drink, Jean."

Jean's parents were staying with her. It had been a worrying time and they were glad that Jean had tonight as a distraction from Raif's departure and her 'condition'.

Boxing Day. Everything – dates, timing, words and images glitzy and utterly wonderful were assembling in Jean's consciousness. She was going to top the bill tonight. She did not need a red carpet because she would be walking on air. She knew a new mate must be near. She could smell the possibility. In fact, Ria had mentioned that her male lodger was recently single again. Jean knew that another man had already been chosen for her by the Lord. The Lord had a habit of making things fall into place for Jean, especially when she was inspired to hit the heights.

When he found her, Jean fancied that the chosen man would love to unwrap her – like a very special, belated Christmas present. How delicious. Jean stifled a bit of a giggle and caught sight of her profile in the mirror again. Every inch of her was kissable. It felt good.

Tonight, 'he' would be delivered to her from somewhere, somehow. Of this, she was sure. It was just a matter of stepping into the appointed limelight at the other side of the A6.

"Yes." Jean said. "I'm looking forward to it. People. People. An occasion. Good conversation. I think this might be it…" Her voice trailed off as expectation thrilled. She dare not add her other images to the verbal list for fear she would make her mother more anxious.

"You will keep calm, won't you Jean? Don't do anything rash or anything. Don't overdo the gin, will you?" her mother said pointedly. "You don't want to be having another turn, do you?"

Jean did not respond to her mother. She did not want anything to spoil her mind's cocktail. Images of the male physique came thick and fast in legion across her thinking. Would he be dark and interesting with male sullenness, or fair and light-hearted with the velvet glove of intellect? Would his testosterone do for her, belt and braces, or would she have to be the initiator, Mother Earth, harlot and saint? It was all too wonderful to imagine. Perhaps the lodger would fit the bill. Thoughts were racing like they do when the Creator of the Universe takes a hand in your destiny.

"Ever upwards," Jean said at last, in answer to her mother's questions, clinging inwardly to her secret prophesy.

Her mother smiled. "And you said the house is nearby. It's grand and detached isn't it? Do you know this person well? Be careful, Jean, won't you?"

"Yes. It's nearby," Jean said remembering the sweeping staircase, picturing herself halfway aloft striking a pose like Norma Desmond. Utterly stunning. There was a pause as she transformed the A6 into Sunset Boulevard in her mind's eye.

"Jean, what are you thinking about?" her mother said, ever troubled by the knowledge that her daughter had been an 'individual' from the cradle.

"My neighbour, Ria, and the wine. It was the Liebfraumilch in my shopping trolley at the Co-op. That clinched it. Her name's Maria, but they call her Ria, and she's German. She saw my bottle. It wasn't a coincidence. It was meant to be. I do tend to attract interesting people."

"Yes, you seem to have the knack."

"I think she's had a fascinating life; so brave, came here after the War. Imagine what the neighbours thought about having the enemy on their doorstep. She married a man who has businesses, you know, and I'll meet neighbours from across the way, her lodger and the other people she knows. They're all in business."

Jean smiled as she reeled off the facts, feeling that it was all so much better than fiction. She was on to a winner at long last. She liked making her mark with her kind of people – the ones that broke the mould – and the party tonight was a new page in her life's book.

It was new. It didn't matter what it was as long as it wasn't boring. It was part of the Lord's plan. It was a way of escaping thoughts of 'the barmaid' and the Mental Health Unit and the medication. Tonight Jean would be her own instructor, life-coach and shrink. The professionals had fallen short yet again. A misguided crew. They had attempted to seize her soul and distort the way she saw the world and her desires. Their drugs would not keep her captive. No they would not. Down the toilet they had gone, but obviously nobody knew that.

"Well, keep your decorum," her mother told her. "Remember, you're still a mother even though Raif's gone. Remember to take your tablets."

Jean had already kicked the inadequacies of the medical profession into touch. Thank goodness she was a woman with know-how, of no mean intellect, and blessed with the sixth sense that hermits had starved themselves to death to attain. And yet this gift was in her and hers for the taking. What a glorious life had been bestowed upon her. Tonight she would use her gift.

"Yes, I'll be fine."

With a last look at herself, lips coral and full, it was time for Jean to go. She was every ounce a desirable creature. One that was well able to catch any cap tossed her way by the right suitor. She wanted to be entertained.

She wanted to be caressed. She wanted to be loved – and she wanted to be solvent. The Lord would provide.

Matching chic-ly casual and expensive with an unshakeable will, Jean bid her parents goodnight.

"Don't wait up," she called, pressing the door shut firmly into position with both hands. She was closing the door on the past. Her tomorrows were just beginning on this Boxing Day eve.

* * *

"I'll walk you home."

It was late. Much later. Jean stood face-to-face with a hard-chested, virile man called Mitchell. He was Ria's lodger. Jean looked into his eyes. His offer was one she could not refuse.

It had been a night etched in time, and Jean had been the life and soul. And here she was with a good-looking man who was separated from his wife, in employment – in management no less – and gagging for her.

Jean was very interested in Mitchell's white collar status in the workplace. She imagined him hiring and firing all and sundry in the shoe factory. He was in charge. That being the case, his earthy, son of the sod look caused her no disquiet. In fact, it became very appealing indeed as the night wore on. After all, a man with big hands and muscular thighs was surely worth a second thought.

"Steady," Jean said, teasing. Mitchell was smoothing his hand across her shoulders and back. Her flesh sang to his touch and, as if bewitched, Mitchell started humming

'Isn't She Lovely'. A Stevie Wonder tape had been playing at the party when Jean arrived, and Mitchell had made a bee-line for her as soon as he laid eyes on her. He was in transit, a lodger in mid-life missing the home comforts a wife supplied.

The 'new couple' were the last to leave the party. They all said their goodnights. Cars moved away. Ria's door was closed and all that was left was the night, the misty glow of a discreet street light, and their breaths meshing together on the cold night air. They stood in the quiet of Ria's porch leaning against the wall and each other. It was lusciously clandestine, just the way Jean liked things with her men – exciting and forbidden, off-beat and bloody marvellous.

"I need to walk you home." Mitchell was straightforward.

"Okay, but my parents are back home, so I don't want to disturb them."

"I'll look after you, and I guarantee they'll like me if they're still up. They'll like me; I can do the garden, I'm good round the house, and I can behave when I have to," he stated.

"Can you? What a pity!" Jean said rolling her eyes, her oval mouth glistening with the lip gloss she had re-applied just before they'd left the party. She always tried to look her best – you never knew.

Her mouth faced his.

"A kiss would be nice," Mitchell said, and inserted his tongue.

Jean steadied herself against the flower trough in the porch. Once anchored, she was able to take in his lips, top and bottom, and his tongue with the suction of a Dyson. It had been a long time since Jean had been joined to any part of the male anatomy. She gave it her all, and Mitchell was immediately very gratified.

His erection, both its rate of growth, and its size startled Jean who was barely able to withhold its girth between her thighs. Thank goodness she'd had the presence of mind to wear knickers this evening. With restraint, assuming the air of an adored woman, she suggested they start walking home as soon as possible.

"Keep a grip," she whispered, sensing he was hot and bothered and on the brink. "Let's get back to mine. I'm not an outdoor type. I like a nice man in nice bed linen – Egyptian cotton usually – and a plumped up pillow.

"That'll do me," Mitchell said already heading towards the A6, and home.

* * *

It was a heady romance topped off with a diamond cluster engagement ring. After more romance, Mitchell moved in. It was only right.

It all seemed so heaven sent. Mitchell and Jean's parents got on like a house on fire. The night they met, he made a point of calling them 'Mum and Dad'. It was all ordained, of course. Far be it from Jean or anyone else to question the Lord's predestined plan. The star-crossed lovers made their pact of passion, pounds, shillings and pence. All that was left was destiny with the living and the dead at the appointed times.

The marriage, a quiet and simple affair, took place at the Registry Office. Not even the children were told. It was important that their father did not know. It could have been tricky with the ex and the groom going head-to-head.

"I love it. I love it when it's splendid," Jean mouthed at her new husband. It was a special day, set apart as she wished. The wedding was a hit. The photographs would have done Tatler proud, not to mention 'Hello' magazine.

* * *

Married life began in a whirlwind but as the months unfolded, the couple's life gave way to a form of routine. It is the normal thing that happens in marriage, but Jean's life was full and there were moments of high-jinks and kiss-and-chase for a while. Then came the so-called sloth routine; the ordinariness of living.

Amidst the long weeks, one day things began to take a turn. There was waning passion, domesticity and uncertainty but one day, out of the blue, Mitchell announced that he had secured a job transfer to Indonesia. A long way from the East Midlands! A satellite shoe factory with markedly cheaper production costs than those in England was to be established and Mitchell had volunteered his services.

"A change is as good as a rest," he said unblinkingly looking Jean's way.

"Yes."

Jean was ready to think of new climes and a different social scene. After a lot of discussion, she convinced her new husband that she should go with him, rather than rely on his return at holiday times. After all, a fine house went with the job and the culture dictated that servants must tend to the occupants.

"I fancy I could get used to a new life," Jean mused. "And I do like a Thai curry!"

Grandeur indeed. Oh the lure of Java – the iconic 1950's cinematic backcloth. It was Jean's for the taking. What an opportunity. And anyway, Jean was already feeling that a boost on the domestic front would be most welcome. She wasn't one for letting the grass grow. Mitchell seemed to be spending less time in the house, working late he always said – another reason why she insisted that she go with him. What a dream – an ex-pat Utopia for the couple would be perfect.

As ever, Jean thanked the Lord that He moved in such a mysterious way, and the wonders He performed in her life.

* * *

The heat and dust, visiting friends, and caring for the servants as any respectable English woman would, quickly filled the days and months and the factory soon began to make money. Mitchell seemed to have a way with the staff, particularly his secretary who was very efficient. He was always at work, but he didn't seem to mind.

The time passed. Jean had novelty in her life and accepted Mitchell's absences. Some nights the workload was so great that he didn't return home. It seemed that business must be thriving.

Still the family ties in the UK were important. Expat through and through, delicious in silk and gloriously different, Jean was called upon to sacrifice her colonial life style for a while. Ever in demand, Jean simply had to fly home to be with her parents in England for a time to assess their health. They grew older in years and she felt she had to be with them as any astute, good daughter would do.

"Yes Mother, I will come home. It's important that I see to things," Jean assured her mother over the phone.

It was important to Jean that she was there at the end. There were things to see to, wills to be checked and so on. Mitchell was insistent that Jean did her duty in England and leave their marital home for as long as she needed to be with her aging parents.

And so Jean returned home to England. She slotted back in with her parents. The months rolled by. There was always plenty to do and Jean was at the helm, making sure that the future was as she wanted.

Then, one day, news from overseas changed her life. Rarely fazed, Jean received a phone call from Indonesia. One which she had not expected.

* * *

"Dead? Mitchell?"

"Yes. Your husband is dead Mrs Thornett."

"Dead? Mitchell?" Jean held the phone closer to her ear, thinking that she must have misheard.

"His body has been found and identified. Mr. Mitchell Thornett. I am very sorry to give you this news." The voice of the Javanese British embassy official faltered a little. Jean didn't know whether it was emotion or a bad line.

"Dead? But I only spoke to him this morning. He said he was going up country for the weekend as it's your national holiday."

"Yes, it is."

A million and one images ram-raided Jean's mind. She changed her facial expression to match what she'd seen on the big screen. Bette Davis was a dab hand at heartfelt grief. It was hard to know what to feel, what to be. It was strange to explore the lack of any sensation. She felt next to nothing, just surprise. Within the persona she assumed, she continued.

"I can't believe it," Jean said, getting the feeling she was following a well-known script. "My husband was such a robust man. What happened? How did he die? Who found him?"

She was living the part. She felt propelled by a kind of cinematic energy. It welled upward from nowhere racing ahead of itself.

There was a silence. The Indonesian official did not speak.

"Well?" Jean pressed fiercely. "Who or what killed him?"

"A heart attack, Mrs. Thornett. I do not have all details, but funeral arrangements need to be in place as soon as you are able."

"Who found him?" she questioned abruptly. Jean could smell a rat. Instinct. A Ray Chandler crime novel, hard-boiled and full on was emerging in Jean's psyche. She assumed the role of a vulnerable and street-wise woman; a dame not to be messed with. "Come on. Spill!" she demanded in a New York drawl. This was blockbuster news indeed.

There was more silence.

"He was with a woman, wasn't he? He died with a woman didn't he? Just tell me."

The official was unaccustomed to the ways of western women, let alone a woman of Jean's calibre. He had never seen American television or English for that matter.

"Yes. We believe it was his secretary."

The image of Mitchell's petite, eager-to-please helpmate drifted into Jean's mind. "Yes, I see. Well, that doesn't surprise me at all. Not one little bit. She was submissive and he was, in her eyes, important. She was fair game."

"I am sorry, Mrs. Thornett. Please accept my sincere condolences."

"Don't be sorry," Jean said, lengthening the drama of it all. She rallied herself for the climactic moment. "You see," she began, making sure she enunciated every word so that the foreigner on the other end of the phone could understand. "You see, my husband liked to have a lot of sex – but not with me."

A longer silence ensued.

At last Jean extracted a contact phone number from the embassy official. She would consult with Mitchell's children from his previous marriage and find an available flight.

"I'll get back to you with details," she said, replacing the receiver.

* * *

It soon dawned on Jean that she was in fact a widow. It was not a role she had ever had to play before.

Her mind processed an array of possible widow's weeds. 'Clothes maketh the woman' was her mantra. She must acquire outfits suitable for this holiday with a difference. Yes, there was the funeral, and she must deal with the corpse, but it would be foolish not to make it into a holiday too. She was mindful that she must become the archetypal British Establishment figure. How would the Queen dress in these circumstances?

Jean determined to spread the news of Mitchell's untimely demise and the manner of his going. She would accept the charity of friends, and then indulge in urgent and comprehensive shopping with her usual panache.

* * *

The funeral took place as planned.

"Thank you. Thank you, all." Jean, revered by the locals, was ever-giving with her upper lip stiff for the onlookers.

Funeral done, there was the Bali holiday to look forward to. She would arrange to meet old, ex-pat friends and go to the beach. However, she had Mitchell's ashes to consider. The problem of the ashes. What was she to do with them? It would be unseemly to take his ashes to the beach with her, and Jean was determined not to lug his urn across Java. There was another problem; the post-funeral beach holiday had been booked with a connecting, internal flight from the mainland to Bali as soon as she had been informed of Mitchell's demise. Widows need a holiday too, but what could she do with the urn?

Jean sipped at her glass of champagne in the airport lounge as she waited for the connecting flight, and considered the conundrum of Mitchell's ashes. The memory of the funeral was still fresh, and she took this time at the airport bar to do a replay. The images of the funeral spilled into her mind's eye again.

She had conducted herself exceedingly well, she thought, with a very British sense of decorum. The entire village had turned out to see her. She had negotiated the ceremony, measured grief, the incendiaries used to burn Mitchell's body, and the stench of kerosene. At one point there was a blow-back because the system was basic. As the body burned on, a breeze lifted his body, causing ash to coat the mourners, their clothes and faces. Jean had swallowed some of the ash blown back, but she did not flinch. It put her in mind of that first deep kiss with Mitchell on Ria's doorstep the night the heavens had declared they must become one flesh, but she stayed poised and swallowed hard.

Maintaining poise came easy. After all she'd had a good teacher. Years of watching Her Majesty had paid off, and her yearning to emulate her know-how had come to fruition. Jean officiated. She took to widowhood. She was a natural. All those adoring eyes native to Indonesia followed her every move. She had awed them. Her job was done.

Ever the pragmatist, and convinced the Lord had a new chapter ready for delving into, Jean squatted in the starting blocks alert for adventure. Life sounded his clarion call, and Jean was not deaf to it.

However, in the interim there was still the problem of Mitchell's ashes. Where could she stow them while she went to Bali and how would she get them back to the UK? She decided not to be a martyr to them. The funeral urn was heavy and ungainly to carry and it was too big to go in a hotel room safe.

"I'm not taking them to Bali. Mitchell wasn't that keen on Bali, anyway," Jean said.

"What will you do with them?" Jean's daughter asked, eyeing the size of the urn. She was accompanying her mother to deal with Mitchell's effects, and she was up for a holiday.

Jean focussed on the urn. She then had a thought. Solutions came to her the way miracles did. She turned to her daughter, making sure not to spill her champagne, and with deliberation, she said;

"Well, there's always the airport 'left luggage' drop-off, isn't there? I can leave him there. I can put him in a carrier bag. Nobody'll know."

* * *

Holidays come to an end, unfortunately. The funeral and the Bali beach holiday had both been successful. The holiday had been a real tonic. Widow had been duly distracted from her grief.

Jean lay back in her seat in the aircraft bound for Heathrow, relaxing herself with a cheeky red wine, avoiding thoughts of the outstanding mortgage she would have to face once home. Yes, the holiday was really over. Jean began to think on the past. The end of her marriage to Raif, the one night stand with Mitchell which turned into marriage, her life as an ex-pat and then his funeral. Her cup of life runneth over indeed.

She looked into her reflection on the glass as she held the wine aloft before she drank from it, the wine goblet smooth and round like a red crystal ball. Jean knew that the Almighty could use any vessel to speak out his will, as he had on many occasions when Jean was in need of a hotline to him.

This was one such occasion. There had been a glitch, a cash-flow problem. Mitchell had neglected to mention to the insurance company that he'd had a triple heart by-pass. Consequently, Jean was in a bit of a spot. No income and a mortgage to pay. And of course, she must live. Why compromise one's shopping habit? And so she hoped Heaven's floodgates would break soon. She had the faith. She waited on His message.

She nestled into her seat and adjusted the position of her feet which were resting on Mitchell. The urn containing his remains could not be stowed in the aircraft hold, and it was too big and heavy for the luggage rack. Jean had slipped the urn into a Mark's and Spencer's carrier bag for fear the Indonesians might eject her from the plane had they known she had brought death on to it.

She took another sip from her glass, suddenly feeling someone at her shoulder as she did so. Then the lavender-scented flight attendant bent down towards her in well-trained manner and enquired as to Jean's comfort.

"Can I help you ma'am?" she said, smiling through what seemed to Jean to be an Indonesian haze. The champagne and the wine had been very good quality. "You have no room for your feet, ma'am. Would you like us to move your bag into the crew cabin?"

"No, it will be fine," Jean answered, balancing her ankles on top of Mitchell.

"Are you certain, ma'am? It would be very bad for you to get the cramp."

At the word '*cramp*,' Jean's irises dilated. The divine lightbulb moment had struck again. She appeared dumbstruck. Most unusual.

"Cramp. Of course," Jean said to herself. "Cramp!" she shouted, looking round as if Jehovah himself would appear.

The cabin crew girl looked confused and scuttled her small frame away from Jean along the aircraft aisle. "Thank you," Jean called gleefully after her.

"What's the matter?" Jean's daughter asked, seeing her mother animated and loud. "Don't scare the crew."

"Listen, daughter of mine. I always said the Lord provides and he just has."

"What?"

Jean Riley

"God has just messaged me," Jean said, breathless with the divine revelation. "He's told me to get in touch with Peter Cramp. You know Peter Cramp, my old flame. Listen, it's all meant to be. Peter Cramp is a bachelor, and the owner of a multiple occupancy building! Think of all the rent that generates."

Jean's daughter shook her head as Jean pressed her buzzer for service. A refill was necessary.

"Come on, a celebration is in order!" she shouted as she stood on top of Mitchell and waved to catch the attendant's eye.

* * *

And the rest is history…

Jean liked the idea of a Canadian wedding and had her sights set on Vancouver Island. Peter Cramp complied. Jean saw to every detail and the heavens bore witness as predicted.

3 In the Shade of Gun Smoke and Mops

"I can't wait to go. It's people, people, people that I want. I need," Jean said in the direction of her husband.

She took stock of her life with Peter. It comprised of horses, boats and guns and one or two other things not worthy of much note. True, they lived a life something akin to the Royals, but Jean was tired of managing Peter's morose downturns. Like Churchill he seemed to have been bitten by the 'black dog' and this was sapping Jean's desire to sparkle. Their social scene had significantly dimmed since Peter had pilfered someone's fenders at the yacht club. Jean was not for accepting society's cold shoulder. No man was worth that. Peter must change or he was out.

As simple as that. The coming weekend in Wales would be the test.

"When we get there I want you to behave. Stay close to me like a wife should. Are you listening, Jean? I don't want you going off and starting things."

Jean ignored Peter's warning born of his possessiveness. The trouble with some men was that they didn't like to be outshone. Peter was one such man. Son of the sod he was, and son of the sod he would remain. Jean feared that his plodding take on life was reducing her natural charisma. An overwhelming urge to wash that man right out of her hair bubbled beneath the surface of her time spent with him.

She sensed the 'black dog' descending on the project in hand again already, but she kept her peace because the proposed hunting weekend in Wales would break the monotony of life with her third, oh-so-glum husband.

The Crossly crowd weren't bad, and Jean felt in dire need of an evening when she could hold sway. She was ready to challenge or stroke the odd male ego or two depending on how the mood took her. She knew something must happen. Mercury was rising.

"I am who I am," Jean said curtly. "There's nothing wrong with making connections, you know. People do speak to each other in company. That's called having a social life. Lighten up for God's sake. You may even enjoy yourself."

That was Jean's last word on the matter. She turned her attention to packing. She thought on quality tweeds for the day and something eye-catching and sophisticated for the evening. Within reason, of course – after all it was only Wales they were heading for, not Balmoral.

* * *

Jean liked to travel. "I hope it's a decent place."

Peter didn't answer. The hunting lodge turned out to be a stone pub in remote Wales. No matter. It was a change for the better, and if the great outdoors were good enough for Her Majesty, they were good enough for Jean. Though, it must be said, Jean would never wear a head scarf as the Queen did when traversing her estate; one had to keep one's individuality at the forefront. Jean determined she would never be one of those middle-aged women who became invisible. That would have pleased Peter, but God had not put her on this earth to please such like as him.

Day one was all active. Trooping, shouting, aiming and guns clacking were the order of the day. It was hands-on and energising. Jean felt buoyed up by the day. Her mood heightened, more so as she did not have to endure Peter ill-at-ease in conversation with those around him.

The day had been full-on, and an evening wide open for possibilities lay ahead. The couple retreated to the bedroom to make ready for the evening social.

"I cocked a few today," Peter mused. He had had a good shoot. He loved his guns – the feel of them, their smell and the kick back they gave him.

"Just a few," Jean said, her mind on the evening that lay ahead, gin in hand.

Jean Riley

Peter liked his guns powerful. He could control them and they didn't talk back. When out and about there was no fancy conversation to plague him. He could stand, look, shoot and walk away at will. There was no opportunity for gaps in conversation which Peter would normally feel the need to fill with embarrassing talk that nobody related to.

Jean gulped in the sense of freedom this imputed to her. This, and the gin, raised her expectations for the evening. Her thoughts gathered momentum. She was gay and talkative and playful adding her jewellery and lipstick top up, barely noticing Peter at all as she made ready for a night to remember. They would be eating and drinking as a crowd. Jean put the finishing touches to herself and eyed her profile with great anticipation.

"Are you ready? Shake a leg, and don't forget when you order at the bar, I want ice. Ice. What's the good of gin without ice?"

Peter barely looked up. Before getting changed, he returned his gun to the wardrobe in the room, lingering longer than needed as he closed the door shut with bowed head.

"You'll get your wish," he said.

He began to get dressed for the evening, but with an irksome awkwardness. He spoke little. Tonight, he would rather have locked the bedroom door and drank in private with his wife near at hand where he could keep the lid on her. That way he would not need to try to join in with the conversations. By keeping Jean separate from other people, particularly men, he could make sure that her mood stayed on an even keel.

He dwelt on the idea that if she took a turn and had to be sectioned, the pub was too remote for a doctor and the police to get to her quickly. Also, he had no idea where the nearest mental health unit was. The night ahead held little charm for him, just the usual anxieties.

Peter found that he was spending more time living in his own head. Human contact was a growing challenge. It was safer alone.

He went through the motions of getting ready. He always looked the part, but tonight he could find no snippet of bravado or anything that normally helped him to get by. For Jean the evening revelries felt promising.

"Are we set?" Jean said with some irritation. "I'm ravenous."

"Just calm down. All in good time," Peter replied, already jaded. Time clicked on. Jean imagined the Crossly crowd waiting for them to make their entrance. Soon she and her husband emerged immaculate with no chinks in the matrimonial armour on show. They descended the stairs and entered what the locals called the banqueting room.

"We're here," Jean called out on the stairs. In energised mood she surveyed the scene downstairs in the pub. The long wooden tables laden with food added a touch of grandeur, made grander still as Jean cut a good figure, well turned-out, with a cheeky glint, somehow younger with a touch of the debutante about her.

"I could eat a horse," she smiled. "But not a whole one."

Her conversation caught the attention of her party and locals alike. Her wit and vivacity interested all who were eligible from gentleman farmer to barman. Conversation and antics ebbed and flowed. Jean was in her element.

Occasionally mid-conversation above the chink of glasses, Jean looked over at Peter. Somehow he seemed diminutive to her. She glanced his way again. He appeared to be getting smaller and more wizened. He glowered in her direction, darkened in his morose self. Jean could look on him no longer, but busied herself adding the political edge, the double entendre and the only glamour in the whole place for every looking eye.

Things started to move faster in her mind. Soon it became very clear that she must open her soul to the destiny the Lord had ordained for her. This evening was the stepping stone to severance which she must tread. Peter's strangle hold on her, and his repeated references to the need to have her sectioned were intolerable. Why should she be incarcerated because she wanted to have fun? What was wrong with being an individual? Jean smouldered to think that her dreary husband had hoodwinked doctors into locking her up in the past. Never again. Off with the old and on with the new. She determined that once she returned home from this weekend away she would begin divorce proceedings.

"He's history," she heard a voice say. It sounded decisive. She liked that. Her thoughts were racing, intermingled with expectation, hunger and a dry mouth.

The evening went by too slowly for Peter. In his mind it would soon be time to call it a day. He knew he would go to the bedroom alone. He would wait for Jean to come later.

"I'm going up now," he said to Jean. "Don't be long."

"I'm staying. I'm having fun. You're a long time dead," Jean answered with a full smile.

"Yes, you are," Peter said with deliberation, making eye contact with his wife for the first time that evening. "A long time dead. Goodnight."

He made his way up the stairs to bed, a defeated man, but for Jean the night was young and she was sensing new beginnings. Her smile widened. One of the locals took her hand. Another drink magically appeared. It was all so good. Life, flux, fulfilment. Soon another would be on her arm. There were new places to go, new experiences to be had. The voices rained in to give her suggestions. Images beckoned, fast-moving and beguiling. There was so much to live for, especially when one was single and available. The divorce could not come too soon as far as Jean was concerned. She looked around her again and caught the barman's eye.

"You forgot the ice and a slice," she said above the tinkling of glasses and the trickle of conversation. The barman saw to her every wish.

Once upstairs Peter shut the room door, sat, and drank above the ripples of laughter and the muted babble of conversation downstairs, which was no less rich for his absence. He rolled his tongue around his mouth tasting the spirit on his lips.

In the pit of his middle-aged thoughts, he continued to drink in the darkness, and waited for his wife.

* * *

Jean Riley

Below him, later on when the eating, drinking and talking were done, Jean whispered a squiffy goodnight to her social companions on the stairs. She knew Peter would be asleep. Sex was out of the question now, of course, and she had no wish to talk, so she walked quietly, avoiding loose floorboards. She made sure Peter would stay asleep – she had no wish to wake the dead.

When she entered the bedroom all was quiet and in darkness. An adept undresser, Jean sidled out of her clothes in the dark and sandwiched herself between the bed covers a good two feet away from her husband at the other side of the bed.

It had been a good day, full of activity in the right setting. Her clothes and talk had been a wild success, and Peter had not disgraced himself apart from his usual bland awkwardness. Jean closed her eyes, satisfied; she was not tired, but knew she must try to sleep. Soon, enveloped in her dream life, all the longings she cradled found their expression. In her dreams she was the unfettered, remarkably interesting girl she always was.

* * *

Sometime later Jean stirred in her sleep. She sensed movement and the sound of breathing. Its rise and fall grew louder and gave way to what Jean thought must be an animal grunting in the room. The grunting gave way to sniffing. The pub was rambling and in the middle of nowhere. Maybe a fox or even a wild boar had got into the room.

Jean stayed iron still beneath the sheet holding her breath in the darkness. She sensed something near her face above her then she heard a click of metal on metal. A dull voice came out of the darkness rasping against Jean's ear. It was a man's voice.

"If I can't have you, nobody can have you."

Her body jolted in the darkness. Jean opened her eyes to make out the outline of Peter's face, his words coming to her from his tightened lips, half-spoken through grinding teeth. She began to pray silently. 'Oh God, don't let him kill me.'

Then there was silence again, menacing in the gloom. Peter was still breathing near her face. Jean smelt the gun, oily and close. Statue-still she waited for God to intervene. He normally did. Without moving she began to mouth words.

"Put the gun down Peter. Put it down now. Put the gun down Peter."

* * *

"She said she needs a party," Ria said looking straight ahead, taking a draw on her cigarette. She had made coffee and invited Jean's old friends to join her. They were worried about Jean and her turbulent times with Peter. The episode with the gun was the talk of the moment. They were all so relieved Peter had not blown Jean's head off. Luckily, Peter had relented.

Jean's friends were loyal and not strangers to Jean's funny, or not so funny, episodes. The three of them were to put their heads together in order to decide what must be done next. Ever since Jean had returned from the hunting weekend in Wales she had been restless, and the phone calls had gained momentum. The phone would ring night and day because Jean seemed to have endless things to talk about. It was hard to keep up. In the midst of one frenetic call, Jean had told Ria that she needed a party. Jean had made that a definite request.

"Jean always likes a party," Elena said smiling. "She likes to dress up."

"No Elena, she said that she 'needs' a party," Ria said with stolid deliberation.

"You know, I thought she was going high again when she rang me. She rang me twice last night. I don't think the weekend was any help," Pam added sagely. "She and Peter are a fiery combination, especially after a few gins."

"She should never have married him. It was not love. It was lust from years ago. I may be German, but lust is common across all cultures." Ria was matter of fact. "I know lust when I see it. The Germans are far more intuitive than the English, but Jean can't resist a good-looking man.

"I think Jean gets bored easily, doesn't she?" Elena smiled again. "Do you think they're really not suited, or is she just high again?"

"I told her she must take her tablets. We all know she can go high when she's stressed about something," Pam said and Elena nodded in agreement.

"What is she stressed about more than usual?" Ria asked.

Pam was unsure whether she should relay what Jean had said. "Well, I don't know whether I heard right, but she said she was frightened that Peter was actually going to kill her."

"Was he just larking about? You know what happens when people drink a lot. The gun – was it real?" Elena's eyes grew wide.

"Yes. Well, it wouldn't have been a toy one on a hunting weekend, would it? She said Peter waited for her to fall asleep, then he pounced on top of her and held his gun to her head, said he couldn't take it any longer."

"Really? Good grief." Elena's eyes grew wider still.

"I'm surprised they haven't killed each other by now. They are always arguing," Ria said, blowing out smoke. The trouble is the English can't communicate. As a sociologist I know these things. Well, anyway, getting back to what I was saying. I like to have parties here. The house is big and I like it to be used, so I've told her to come Saturday, so you will all come too."

All nodded their agreement with anticipation. The party was planned. Each wondered whether Peter might bring his gun to the party but no one voiced this.

* * *

Party time. Most unusually Jean was late. Those in the know sincerely hoped that Peter had not shot her in the interim.

"I hope she isn't lying dead somewhere," Elena said. "She's never late."

Elena and Pam kept looking towards the door anticipating Jean's appearance. Elena speculated that

Jean Riley

Jean would resurrect her cruise wear or, knowing Jean, a new outfit may have been bought especially for the party tonight.

"I know Jean likes sequins. There's that lovely pale blue dress she has, and her matching bag was lovely," Elena said tidying away discarded napkins.

"I wonder where she's got to." Pam knew Jean's habits, and being late was very out of character.

"She wanted the bloody party, and she's not even here," Ria said, savouring her Liebfraumilch. "She's the star of the bloody gathering. Late. You must be on time, my mutti used to say. Jean will be making sure she makes her entrance."

Then above the din, the sound of Jean's greeting caused every eye to look towards the door.

"Darlings, I'm here!"

Silence. Nobody moved or spoke. The sight of Jean silenced the whole gathering. Ria was the first to move and speak. She lit another cigarette, still looking at Jean and muttered, "She looks bloody daft. The English are mad."

"It's me darlings, I'm here. I've come to make a clean sweep of things," Jean called out even louder, brandishing a mop above her head.

Every eye was wide and looking at Jean. All were stunned. The sight of her amazed even her seasoned friends accustomed to her episodic behaviour. There she stood with Hilda Ogden head gear, curlers to boot, and with a nylon overall and a mop bucket clanking. She held it aloft whilst rubber gloves dangled from her belt. Dusters, liquids, sponges and a broom handle sporting a fine mop head were her accessories. These bits of equipment, she swiped at will to all who looked aghast.

Elena was the first to speak. "Jean, why are you dressed like Mrs. Mop?"

Jean lifted her head high, and with full red lips declared her intentions. "Because, because, because ladies and gentlemen I am making a clean sweep of my life. I'm washing away the past. I proclaim the death of my third marriage, and so dear friends I am here today to throw it out. Yes, I am washing that man right out of my hair, my life, my all. I am a walking symbol. I have cleaned up my life and next, dear comrades, I will clean up the world. We must clean, sweep and sanitize and oust the old and on with the new."

"Jean, calm down a bit. Where are your tablets, and where's Peter?" Pam asked calmly.

"Gone, gone, washed away. All gone and there's more to come."

It did cross their minds that Jean may have shot Peter, and that he may be lying dead at home, but nobody voiced this. It would have been too terrible, but well within the realms of possibility.

At this, Jean put down her bucket, stood boldly and with the look of Joan of Arc before her nation, she raised her hands, grabbed her overall, threw it open and revealed the emblem that lay beneath. Again the party fell to silence.

Jean thrust forward her chest. There her white T-shirt appeared sporting large, balloon-like bosoms painted on with the reddest nipples imaginable standing prominent as big as poppies.

Stunned smiles appeared around the room. Most people didn't know quite how to react. Jean continued to model her glamorous washer woman persona. Her exaggerated red lips matched the sexy red of her suckable nipples exactly.

Elena looked at Pam and said quietly, "I wonder why she's painted nipples on her Mrs. Mop tee shirt?"

Pam stared at Jean again, and with a thoughtful look she replied, "Well, perhaps she thinks she's a 'dolly' tub – dolly bird, sort of thing"

Elena nodded a sort of understanding nod, and decided the best thing to do was to act normal.

4 *In the Shade of the Millennium*

Jean was an alien in Norway. She did not have her suitcase, she had no clothes. Peter had seen to that. He'd gone. It was not the first time that a husband had abandoned her. She consoled herself with her thought that once she had found the Concorde, her clothes would also be found and the real mission could begin. Meanwhile, she must get from A to B in a taxi to make it all happen.

The taxi driver looked at Jean through his mirror and began to speak to his interesting passenger. Jean looked relaxed, but she had ideas aplenty on the trigger. It was all high energy thinking.

"I hear Beckham from your country can bend the ball," the taxi driver said. "He scores good goals. We don't have good footballers in Bergen!"

"Yes, and his wife is Posh Spice, you know," Jean said. "They are the golden couple in England. Utterly marvellous. Such wealth. They live in splendour. They used to say I was one half of a golden couple, you know. I was Liz Taylor to my husband's Burton… and still am in many ways!"

The taxi driver smiled and looked at Jean again through his mirror on to the back seat of his cab. Jean was not his average passenger. Resplendent on the back seat, smothered in a fur coat, he saw Jean thrust her inhaler into her mouth again. She coughed in a chest full of its contents. She tilted her head back, eyes closed, and luxuriated in the effects of the drug. The transportation was bliss. She could hear her heart beating even above the radio in the cab.

Slowly the urge for her mission returned and grew apace again within Jean. "I feel it. I feel it!" she said aloud, half to herself and half to the Creator. On the cusp of the Millennium, the planetary formations were moving into position and Jean knew she too must play her role. She had not chosen to become the Messiah's mouthpiece; greatness had been thrust upon her again and, as always, she would be on standby ready to harness every fibre of body and soul for the greater good.

"How far?" Jean asked again, restless, on the trigger for the mission. She pulled her coat around her again, leaned forward and looked out of the window, eyes towards the heavens. "Still no sign of that bloody Concorde! I've been looking for it for days. It should be here waiting for me. It has been assigned for me. All I can think of is that this country's air traffic control is inefficient and not letting it in. How far are we from Bergen airport?"

"We're just two minutes away, but I don't think Concorde is due here today, though. Have you got the date wrong, do you think?" The taxi driver was trying to be polite.

"Wrong? Oh my good man, very *right*! Believe me I have the date very right. Everything is in perfect harmony. The heavens have decreed. The Messiah cometh indeed he doth," she smiled a knowing smile, and pouted just a little. "Don't you see, don't you understand? Soon there will be peace in the Middle East. All we have to do is wait for the Millennium and the Second Coming as ordained two thousand years ago, and I am the instrument chosen to consummate it. God meeteth Man. Yes, you are looking at the Lord's Right Hand right here in your taxi. But, but I need the bloody Concorde to appear. Without that we remain in the throes of the Evil One."

"I see," the cab driver said, not seeing at all. Perhaps all the English were eccentric.

Enough said, Jean took a deep-throated pull on her inhaler and sank back in irritation on to the back seat. Animated and exhausted in turn, her heart was beating rapidly. She closed her eyes, hummed a few bars from Holst's Planet Suite then sprang forward as the taxi turned into the airport drop-off

Once inside the airport building, Jean set out to investigate. She walked with as much deliberation as she could muster, the fur coat flapping against her bare legs in folds. The sounds of loud haler voices delivering sing-song messages about times and world destinations, the blipping of electronic devices, the glare and clink of the duty-free, the kaleidoscopic mess of colour and shine all contributed to her moment. All the smells, noises and sights were part of Jean's fanfare heralding the coming of the Concorde, and her subsequent debut on the stage of world events.

"Where do the VIPs go?" she asked a passing stranger. There was no reply.

She was unsure whether the Messiah himself would appear or whether indeed she actually was the Messiah, albeit female and, at this moment in time, bare-legged to boot under her fur coat. She walked then she stood to stare intermittently.

This cacophony of sounds, smells and sights were a cocktail of delight and so vivid. It must be savoured. And the thought of what was to come must be savoured too. Jean took her time examining every face, every detail, wide-eyed as if she was seeing the world for the very first time. This was not just an airport, but the world that God had created in microcosm. She marvelled at the fact that He had chosen her.

However, euphoria was not long lasting. "Get thee behind me!" Jean spoke in a guttural voice. Thoughts from elfin, almost demonic creatures spiked their way into her thoughts every so often. She grated her teeth and swore under her breath again hating her current husband with every grind.

Peter had not delivered her suitcase to her. He had left her isolated in Bergen whilst he had jollied off to Voss.

There was no compassion in that tousled haired, brute of a man. "Bloody idiot," she growled. Determined, she ditched the thought of Peter and got on with the making of history. Then, what she imagined to be the voice of the Lord came like the ringing of many waters from the inside of the fiord.

"Excuse me Mrs… er, is everything all right? My colleagues were concerned about you." Jean looked up to see that the Lord had sent the military to look after her. A man was speaking to her. He was enormous. Jean cast her eyes over his torso and Norwegian legs. Here was a handsome man in uniform with sideburns offering company and succour.

"I'm looking for my Concorde," Jean stated, matter-of-fact.

"Concorde?"

"Yes, Concorde. Where are your colleagues?" Jean asked knowing full well that the eyes of God in the form of CCTV had brought this official man with clout to locate her Concorde and get her on it forthwith. "Has it just landed?"

"No. No Concorde here today. The airport is too small. You seem to be wandering, and we wondered if you'd come with us to sort out what needs to happen."

Jean nodded a knowing affirmative nod in answer. Without blinking she concurred, of course. The Plan must be fulfilled. This seraph in uniform was in on it all. When God cannot come himself he always sends an angel. She had had that message on good authority many a time over the years. She walked with purpose alongside what

Jean Riley

Jean grew to understand was a police officer. Two more appeared and with clockwork precision they got into a waiting car. The journey to the police station was not long, but it was spectacular. It was only fitting, Jean thought as she veered through the streets of Bergen, strapped into a police vehicle with three big men.

"I like your style," Jean said eyeing the profiles of these Norwegian men who had entered her life. She wanted to know everything about their Scandinavian lives. These men were sons of the earth and, as she regarded them, they morphed into Peter, James and John – the three most important of the Lord's disciples. They had been with Christ when God the Father had transfigured him. How apt, Jean thought, dwelling for some time on the sensation of becoming God-like.

"I like what I see," she said, almost in dinner-party mode, enjoying the rush of it all.

"The UK has David Beckham. He can bend the ball to score, I think," said the largest of the three men. Jean nodded in agreement, still entranced. She knew nothing of football, but was at home with the talk of men.

She began to view the city's sights, the colours. She heard the siren, bathed in the dancing lights and felt part of the Norwegian people wearing their shoulder pads and European suits and hessian bags. The motion of the car made all swim together in one fabulous celestial soup. "Yes, I like your style," Jean said again.

Soon they reached the police station.

* * *

"We need to search you Jean. For your own safety. Take your coat off please, and put your arms out." The police station was dark and wooden. Officers with open Norwegian faces spoke with her.

"But I can't. I haven't got the time. I have a job to do. I must get on".

"Remove your coat now please. Your personal items will be saved in the safe. This is our procedure. You then go on to have a shower. It is our rule that you have to have a shower before entering the cell."

The syllables spoken by the Norwegian desk sergeant were clipped and extremely fine Standard English, Jean thought. However, she could not seem to make him understand that Concorde was waiting for her somewhere, and she must get on it to be ready for what was to come. She had a mission to lead. Also, there was the small matter of her nudity beneath her fur coat.

"Take off your coat please so we can do the search."

"I've told you I can't."

"But you must do this, now please."

The whole thing was becoming tiresome. "I concur!" Jean shouted then thrust back her head, chin held high. With a resigned look and a hint of a pout Jean held out her arms, then thrust both hands into her pockets and lifted each side of her coat aloft, wide open for all to see. Seven pairs of eyes involuntarily fell on to Jean's crotch and bare legs as the coat flapped open. All fell silent. There was no movement in the police station. The officers simply stood aghast.

Jean Riley

"Extraordinary," said the desk sergeant, breaking the silence as Jean stood, arms outstretched in the shape of a cross baring all.

"Yes, my purpose *is* extraordinary," said Jean with resounding surety. "This Millennium and the coming of the Messiah *are* truly extraordinary."

There was a clicking of fingers and a woman police officer stepped forth in a scurry to gather up the flapping coat. She covered Jean's lower half with business-like efficiency, trying to make her decent.

The Norwegians, still silent, were more than a little relieved.

* * *

"Where are you taking me?" Jean asked.

The staircase in the police station was steep and creaky and was made of rich, dark, Norwegian wood. Jean descended it with her followers into the cell area beneath the city of Bergen. They told her there would be a shower. She must have a shower then be led to the cell for the night. No matter. Jesus was in the desert for forty days and forty nights and was tempted by the devil – or was it Moses in the desert for forty days? The detail didn't matter as long as Jean fitted in with the ordained plan. This was not a punishment; this incarceration was a blessing. A means to an end. As yet mankind looked through a looking-glass dimly, but soon Jean was to look directly into the face of God.

"Take your time, Jean," a voice said in impeccable English. Jean leant on the arm of the huge Norwegian policeman, allowing him to steer her passage towards what lay beneath.

She was cold when she entered the shower near what was to become her cell. She had given in protesting, and decided to have the shower on the promise of a Ryvita later. She looked upwards to the nozzles and soon streams of water began to jet on to her skin. As the water cascaded on to her head and body, Jean used the time to recall what had happened over the last week. It was an interlude where she could take stock.

Peter's face came back into her inner vision. She, Peter, and holidays never seemed to work. She remembered the rough sea and the misery of the ferry. She thought about Peter making sure he got his 'two for the price of one' at the bar, and all the other paltry disappointments and boredom of her life with him. Sex was robotic and cumbersome and put her in mind of a terrier desperate to get at the ferret.

"Hit me with your rhythm stick!" Jean shouted over the noise of the shower, laughing at the thought of Peter's sex face. There was no ear nibbling, no biting or teasing. Sex with him was like the banging of the plumbing when the heating comes on. He could do it, but he couldn't seem to feel it. Orgasm eluded Jean. Always. When she had insisted their boat should be called "Foreplay", the irony was completely lost on poor Peter, and he agreed.

"Idiot!" she grunted. The memories were too much. The fact that Peter told their friends and more than one psychiatrist that Jean was mentally ill was ludicrous to her way of thinking. "I'm an unfulfilled woman," she shouted, hating the memory of her bedroom moments with Peter.

She recalled the gun he had held to her head when she was in bed on the shooting weekend. She concluded that *he* was the psychopath, albeit with the best buns she had ever set eyes on in her whole life on any man. There was something sex-like about him at times. It all depended. They, the buttocks, weren't fake unlike him. Even so, he must go. She must sever ties. Now that the big event, ordained from on high, was close it was only proper Jean be rid of him.

"There are controls on the wall to alter the flow of water if you want to," a voice called, but Jean ignored it. She enjoyed the force of the water in the shower. It took her breath away and made her heady. It was like soporific music, loud, exacting her soul. She put herself under the water's force, drunk with exhilaration. She let it overtake her. Today was a special day; the year 2000. Every wind and storm had battered the winter of her Millennium experience. Her thoughts raced back over the last week.

Peter had persuaded her that they should travel across Switzerland and Norway. She thought back to the Christmas trip to Switzerland. It had been ordinary beyond belief. There had been a dearth of crackling log fires, and there was always the plodding, peevish intention that Peter would have her sectioned and put away in the asylum again whenever he could. She used to wave the accusing finger at her.

"They'll lock you up. I only have to say."

That was his threat. Little did he know that she preferred the company of lunatics rather than be with him in his bargain-basement of a world. The New Year, the

Millennium in Bergen would be life changing, and here she was on the cusp of catastrophic change for her – for the world. "Glorious," Jean said with gravity.

"Ready to come out?" the female police officer called above the noise of water. It continued to beat down on to Jean's head like hail on a canopy. Soon, she mused, her suitcase would arrive and she would be able to smarten up. She would put on lipstick. She fancied that an in-depth conversation with an intelligent man in the shape of a Norwegian psychiatrist would be in order. She imagined him with white hair wearing a polo neck sweater, erudite and fascinated by her. He would indulge her on his couch just like Freud had done with his close, middle-aged, well-heeled women. It would be such a marvellous send off. She may even allow the Norwegian psychiatrist to medicate her if he proved to be the man she hoped he would be. Her thoughts gathered pace again.

When her communion with Herr Doktor was done, she would go on to meet the Messiah at the time appointed and the rest would be history. History indeed. Perfect. The year 2000. She imagined the stroke of midnight marking the Millennium through the muted sounds of her soap-filled ears. The vision of the end of the world flicked across the back of Jean's eyelids too as she held them tight under the running water. The dead would rise from their graves and everything would be justified as it was written in prophecy. The stroke of the Millennium was upon her and it was glorious.

As she lathered up, using Norwegian soap in the shower next to her prison cell, Jean did wonder what the Messiah would actually look like. Would he appear in white linen at the trumpet call? She did have a strong intuition that the Messiah was probably herself anyway. Or would the Lord alter her vision and surprise her in some way? He had a habit of doing that.

"Come on out Jean. Your finger ends will be like prunes. You are now very clean. Eat now. Would you like cold meat with your Ryvita?" a voice called through the torrent.

"Oh, yes please," Jean answered, dripping on the wooden floor, with sudden interest. "How very Norwegian. How very authentic."

* * *

Time passed. It was an unreal passing of time.

Time must have passed, though Jean did not remember when she began to realize that her mission had come and gone. It was January 2000. The world had not ended, and Jean had not died. The dead had not been raised from their graves. The trumpet had not sounded.

Her spell in the psychiatric hospital in Bergen had proved to be life-changing. Jean had been treated like a queen. Alas, all good things must come to an end, and now she must get back to England. She fervently hoped that Peter had not seized her car. Somehow she must get from the airport, once the plane had landed and head for the ferry terminal. There, she hoped, her car would be waiting intact.

Settling into the aircraft in Bergen, homeward-bound, Jean looked across to her neighbour in the next seat. She felt his arm against hers. The sensation was pleasing. There was something liberating about being in the air suspended over the universe with a man close by. The take-off, and the swell and dropping due to turbulence, added a bit of spice to the trip. Jean was in her element and, ever sociable, asked her companion, "Have you been in Bergen long?"

"A week or so. I've been here on business, but it will be good to get back to the UK."

He had dark eyes and spoke with purpose. Jean held the gaze of this man she had been seated next to. She noted the cut of his suit and his watch. He was very clean shaven, and he put her in mind of the archetypal dapper man. Here she was, sitting next to a man of the world; a man who could doubtless do the Times Crossword unlike Peter Cramp. Peter Cramp – another husband she must dispel to history as soon as she could, once back in England.

"How long have you been in Bergen?" her travelling companion asked.

"Twenty-one days," Jean answered with a fleeting memory of her time on the psychiatric ward she had recently left.

"That's very precise."

"Yes, I was… well, let's just say I was detained," Jean said, determined not to mention her twenty-one day section. She didn't want her companion to think he was sitting next to a mad woman. The memory of the police officers eyeing her flesh when she had opened her fur coat was a little disturbing, but Jean banished the memory quite easily.

"Nothing serious, I hope."

"No… I had to do some research, that's all. Into health services in Norway."

"That's interesting. I've heard health care is very good in Norway."

Jean nodded in agreement, and started to scrutinize her companion even more closely. Here was a man of means who could string a sentence together, unlike her absent husband and with any luck, a gin and tonic would be on the cards and most welcome.

There was no doubt in Jean's mind it would all come to fruition. Soon, she would be single. The plan to bring peace to the new world of the Millennium was also still afoot, but momentarily suspended. The Lord's timing was always perfect. The psychiatric hospital in Bergen had proved to be life-giving. It had saved her from Peter. It had provided asylum from the cold, Norwegian outdoors. Her pneumonia had passed. She could now breathe without the continuous nebulising. She was, once more, a vessel fit for the Lord to use as he would. She knew something lay in store for her. The unravelling of God's predestined plan would come soon, she was sure.

Jean sat with a certain aplomb, well dressed, bejewelled and ready to taste life's juices again. And here was a man on her unscheduled journey with whom she had clicked. Without a doubt the Lord was still at work.

"Would you like a drink?" he asked.

"That would be nice, very nice indeed," Jean responded. "Very nice," she said again slowly looking into her companion's eyes. She looked at his hairline and designer glasses.

The hours slipped by in lush warmth cradled in the rhythmic hum of the aircraft's air conditioning. Conversation with her fellow traveller was delicious, and Jean felt a stirring which she could not deny. It seemed that so much was fitting into place again. She recalled the labyrinth of experiences which had brought her to this point in time with this man who liked red wine, Champagne on occasions and had a weakness for smoked salmon. It seemed rather marvellous.

Landing time drew near. Soon Jean would be in an airport miles from home with no way of accessing her car at the ferry terminal. With customary relish Jean besought the Lord for an answer. She withdrew to the toilet to commune with the Rock of Ages.

Dear Lord, as you know, the psychiatrist wouldn't let me go back by boat for fear I jump over the side. Well, you made that decision happen, and you know the upshot is I can't get to my car at the ferry port. So, Lord, send me a saviour. Come yourself, if you will. If not, send me a saviour because I want to get to my car before Peter gets his hands on it. So, if you can see your way to putting the last piece of the jigsaw into the miracle of your Millennium I would be really thankful. Amen.

* * *

The pilot managed a steady landing with a fast half-turn which mustered the adrenalin.

"Pleasure to have met you, Jean," said her flight companion as he pulled his briefcase from the rack on to the seat below. The engines whined to a stand-still.

"Yes. I've enjoyed our time together." Jean spoke slowly, and hesitated to move along the aisle to exit.

"Don't look so glum. Nobody died!" her companion told her, sensing her reticence.

"No. The thing is I have to get to the ferry terminal to pick up my car. It's been there for three weeks and I'm worried about the whole business." Jean looked directly at her companion. Unabashed, she felt heat strike through her core. The aftermath of the drink, or maybe the Hand of the Almighty touched her then at that point. She knew. She knew His plan was about to be consummated.

"I have a suggestion," her companion said lightly. "They're sending a car for me, so I can drop you off."

That was it. There was the miracle she had sought. Jean mouthed a silent 'thank you'. She reached out to thank her dark stranger, feeling the sinews of his body beneath his suited torso. She felt the woman in her rise.

And so they made the last leg of their journey. Very soon in the distance Jean set eyes on the wasteland of the dock yard. There in the middle, isolated, but fully in-tact stood her car.

"Thank you, thank you," Jean repeated, her eyes wide and receptive. "Maybe we will meet again. I will be divorced soon. Anything is possible."

"Yes," her companion smiled. "Take care."

Jean waved him into the distance, and with the elegance of Grace Kelly she stepped into her car. It started first time. Wonderful. She drove out of the dock land car park, bound for home and the single life – her sure quest in the new Millennium all divinely inspired, of course.

5 In the Shade of the Palace

"Go away!" Jean shouted with all the force she could muster.

It was like being buried alive in a biscuit tin. She woke instantaneously and lay waiting, waiting. She hated caravans and here she was laying in one waiting for yet another seagull to crash land on to its tin roof. They came in droves, thudding, banging, squawking – even speaking strange tongues at times. Jean was unsure whether she should tune in or tune out. The mobile phone wasn't helping either. Her new purchase had meant that Jean had truly 'gone global'. As the holiday progressed, more and more voices were coming through the phone, anything electrical, and the seagulls. Even the dog had got in on the act. And there was Pam.

"There goes another," Pam said, stating the obvious. She, too, laid flat, waiting and listening in another dark corner of the mobile holiday home where she had made her bed out of Jean's earshot. The 'break' had not been a cheery experience so far.

"Yes," Jean answered, the sound of Pam's voice indistinguishable from the conspiring seagulls. Disgruntled by the winged harpies above her head and her less than glamorous surroundings, she answered her companion in curt manner. "It's like being in a tin coffin. Every time they land, they bang another bloody nail in."

"There goes another," Pam said waiting for the next one to land.

Pam was not relishing the day ahead. A change had come over Jean and Pam feared in her waters that it was probably not a change for the better. Jean had been doing so much talking and walking barefoot on the beach and pavements. And there was the sleep deprivation due to the seagulls banging down like jets on a runway. Pam hoped for the best, but she was worried about the dog and Jean. She veered away from challenge and tried what she thought was the subtle approach. "Weather not looking too good again. I wonder if we should call it a day and head back early, Jean?"

"I wouldn't mind a chance of scene. It's gone on a bit, hasn't it?" Jean pondered, ready for the off.

In truth, she'd had her belly full of the bog-standard British beach holiday on a shoe string. She wanted out. She wanted life. She wanted bells and whistles. She had an affinity with the Royals and she believed she was selling them and herself short. She could not turn a blind eye to what stirred in her bowels any longer. She had an inkling that Her Majesty needed her. That being the case, she must go. It went without saying.

Jean emerged from her boxed bed, dark in mood. She moved slowly, eyes intent and expressionless like Lady Macbeth but without the dagger. The convenient cupboards, the gas rings, the incidental paraphernalia used by happy campers assaulted and restrained her proper self. She moved towards the chemical toilet away from the voices of Pam and the seagulls. Soon there would be a cup of bland tea and more incessant talk of seagulls. It was getting to crunch time and Jean knew that soon she must make a move.

The serenity of the toilet was heaven sent. Here she could sit and tune in, and the momentum would build – of that she was certain. Her brain receptors throbbed with longing and expectation. Her Majesty's Secret Service had been sending messages. She knew she must respond. It was all about duty. Jean knew she would be chosen – it was just a matter of when. She must turn her thoughts' trickle into a cascade and move upwards into her next creative phase. She knew she must be on her metal as code-breaking would probably be her bread and butter over the coming weeks. She was no stranger to Bletchley Park. She had circumvented its corridors many a time in her thinking. And of course the Telegraph crossword kept her hand in between missions.

It was now all about getting the details into place. She must concentrate. Currently the detail was coming randomly and racing, but she had faith she would unscramble the messages when the time decreed it. She was ready.

Soon Jean's engagement lifted a gear. She fixed on an escape route from the caravan park in Burnham-on-Sea. Priority number one. She thought about the white tin caravans in neat rows like head stones in a cemetery. She felt she had honoured the dead and the hangers on for long enough, and now she must bite on life for all she was worth. It was about self-survival and the future of the nation.

"How soon can we be ready?" she shouted to Pam.

She imagined her motorway passage. She could already feel her car's throttle and the vibration under her buttocks as her vision gathered force. Like a bat, she would drive out of hell. Too right she would.

"As soon as you like," Pam had already packed.

"Okay," Jean called, thoughts consumed by her persona incognito. "Be with you in a minute."

Jean recalled that her relationship with World Peace was well-documented. Of course it was and if Her Majesty required her service, she would don her Diplomatic hat and blaze a trail without question. The sooner the better. Locations she must visit broke through in wired lights which flashed as she joined the dots. She felt a total at oneness with Churchill in the War Cabinet offices and wondered if he too would be in on this particular job that lay ahead. However, knowing her expertise, it would probably be her alone steering proceedings. It was almost clear now. The circuit on the fuse board illuminated first

Hampton Court, then Westminster, and then of course, Buck Palace. She had been given the green light. She would dress quickly, deal with less important things and then sally forth.

"There goes another one Jean," Pam shouted. "Did you hear that one thud down? It must have been wearing boots. It's like being in the War all over again, isn't it?"

Jean pursed her lips and narrowed her eyes. "Yes, it is, it bloody well is," Jean whispered. "In more ways than one."

* * *

"What time did you say it was taking off, Jean?" Pam shouted above the boom of the car stereo.

"What?" The scenery was flying by in the noise of radio and car engine.

"What time… Concorde… taking off?"

"What?" Jean shouted about the din. Her eyes faced the road, hardly blinking, her heel close to the floor on the accelerator pedal, the blasts of continuous noise intensifying her single-mindedness. Pam had wanted to get straight back home to the Midlands, but Jean had begun to rapture about Concorde again and so they must head for Heathrow. Concorde was centre stage on the international news front, and so it was only fitting that Jean should be there too.

"Jean, turn the music down! Where are we now? Jean!"

"Heathrow, Richmond, somewhere, but I've heard Hampton Court is splendid this time of year," Jean grinned. "Charles does the rounds and he knows his plants. I have a penchant for Hampton. My penchant is being tickled, Auntie Pam. You are game, aren't you? Come on Pam, good God, there's more to life; Concorde is a one-off, Hampton Court is stupendous this time of year. If we get to Hampton Court we could stand in Concorde's flight path and get the full brunt. I want it to be bloody marvellous, Pam. That is why the good Lord put us on this earth to share in the wonder. The awe and wonder dear Pam. You can't get Concorde in the Hampton Court setting on tap. The eyes of the world will be looking. At it. At us, Pam."

"He talks to them," Pam said with surety.

"What? Who talks to what?" Jean retorted absent-mindedly still in the thrall of the aeronautical miracle she was soon to share.

"Prince Charles talks to plants. He swears it makes them grow. You only have to look at High Grove."

"Trees Pam. Trees. He talks to the bloody trees," corrected Jean with zeal, accustomed as she was to directing people. "Anyway, we're talking about the Concorde. The Concorde. A new creation. Do you never yearn to be lost in a great moment, Pam? Try it. Try," she said with irritation. "Life can be bloody marvellous, you know. I wouldn't change a thing. Not really. I'll take anything as long as it's not boring!"

Jean emphasised the word 'boring' and hoped that she'd made her point. She had grown weary always having to be the catalyst for others to see that life could be more than just a routine. 'Have a dose of enchantment. Sugar the bloody pill for God's sake,' she thought to herself.

Pam had to face the fact that Jean was high, sky high, and so her priority would be to try to steer the situation, Jean, and herself to safety. But how?

Jean looked upward and felt that she heard the plane engines ripping at the sky line, Thor in the distance defying the natural order of things. She gulped, blotting out the ordinary, meditating only on the greatness of the moment, experiencing an overwhelming compulsion to speak in tongues. After all, all things were created through Him.

"Oh yes, it was trees, I think. Anyway, Jean it's getting late. I do feel we should be getting back." Pam didn't alter her intonation. The world stage wasn't really her thing. Hopefully, she'd be home for nine o'clock. She might make it in time to watch her favourite detective. Anyway, if she got back a bit later there was always TV 'catch-up' which was free.

* * *

Home again and alone, Jean pranced, bare-footed swaying and keening. She could not settle. She could not sleep or eat. The music blundered and soared through the twilight, the darkness, through the blackness of an inky sky and then into blinding, white light. Great orbs leapt clashing and missing in wrenching disharmony and then miraculous cohesion. The shapes of the planets, fruitlike then elongated, swung through the heavens with the ease of primates scaling the heights and riding the depths. Jean revelled in the enlightenment given to her senses through

Holst's Planets. Still, the music took her again and again, body and soul until she must sit down heady from the movement her body and mind had enveloped.

Electrified, in less than twenty four hours of being back in her own home, Jean knew that she must turn tail and return to London. Pam would not like it, nor would the others, but she must head back to London. The Concorde had been one thing, the Queen was quite another. Mission was, as yet unaccomplished. She must see her monarch.

The movement came to an end. The stereo clicked into silence. That silence gave authority to Jean's decision to return to London. Her Queen had summoned. 'Nough said.

Within two hours Jean lapped the motorway, middle lane, accompanied by dog, music and a diplomatic *raison d'etre* which would be lost on Joe Public. This was special. This was hush, hush. This was the culmination of years standing in the royal wings, studying, understanding the inner turmoil of the Windsors. Her Sovereign never faltered and neither would she. Duty was everything and the crashing realisation that she was so crucial to the wellbeing of the British Royal Family left Jean quite breathless if she would dwell on the idea for too long.

"Nearly there!" she said to Coco, who looked at his mistress, panting with pink tongue out and drooling.

* * *

"Excuse me. I said, *excuse me*. Where is the Mall? The Royal Mall. Quickly please, I haven't time to beat about the bush. I'm on the trigger re. Her Majesty and she's waiting."

"Er, I think Buckingham Palace is up there, but its Sunday so I don't think cars go up there today." The bemused tourist did his best to be polite faced with Jean and dog in arms.

"And where can my dog drink?"

"I think Westminster Cathedral has a café in the basement. That's near you. Maybe, you can get water there."

With dog in clutch-bag mode, Jean, bare-footed and not a penny in her pocket, left the car and descended to the café for water. A Christian woman, goodly in sensible skirt and ironed apron, was only too glad to speak with Jean, and she supplied water in a dog bowl that she happened to have at the ready.

Back on street level, with refreshed vigour, Jean put her foot down, heading for the Palace very gratified that her visit to Westminster had coincided with a public servant shift change-over. She cast her eye towards mainly large men of the Commonwealth dressed in yellow, high visibility jackets. An army of traffic wardens looked directly at her, stopped in their tracks, but none actually ventured forward to speak with her or fine her. This bolstered Jean's mood, for she knew full well that they must have been tipped off. It was a great feeling to have diplomatic immunity with open access to the by ways of Her Majesty's capital. Oh that Wolsey, Thomas A. Becket and Jean's other predecessors had had the same privilege. How the course of history could have been changed, she pondered.

Jean Riley

* * *

Jean looked into the gloom. The Palace seemed ghoulish and ethereal in the night. "Hello, hello!" she shouted, not able to see properly. "Hello! Anybody there?" she called again.

Jean had seen crop circles in the countryside on television documentaries. She was fascinated by the perfection of the arc made by nature, but she had never seen a man-made one comprising of bulk head lights until this evening outside Buckingham Palace. She gazed at the spectacle under cover of darkness. She decided to ignore it as she was intent on gaining entry to the Palace and resumed her position staring into the Palace behind the railings. All was still, not a lantern bearer. Not even the faintest sound of a corgi barking across the night even though Coco, dog-like, was nosing his way into their territory.

"Oh. Very nice," Jean said. "Oh, yes."

She had the sensation of men's hands pushed underneath her arm pits. It was all quite something. Infused, she swayed backwards smelling leather. They were hands, big hands, strong in black leather gauntlets. They almost lifted her aloft and would have done, but for Coco. He was comfortable on Jean's bosom between the railings and the Metropolitan Police.

"Hello," Jean said. "So glad you're here. You can give me some information. Why is the Palace not floodlit? It's very dark. Any Tom, Dick or Harry could scale the railings and infiltrate Her Majesty's chamber." Jean was really quite put out by the risk factor she was bringing to the attention of the police officer.

"Funny you should say that Madam. We were concerned by your presence. Is that your vehicle?" He raised his gauntlet and pointed. Jean turned and her eye followed the direction he pointed out. It led towards the urban crop circle she had wondered about a little earlier. She squinted to see with the help of the squad car head lamps. She could just about make it out. She saw her own car standing illuminated, haloed at gun point with gaping boot, doors and bonnet.

"No need to worry. That's my car, officer. I'm here to see Her Majesty, but you see there's been a problem with synchronisation somewhere along the line. Most unusual. Normally it's like the crest of a wave. Is Her Maj in residence?" Jean asked moving from bare foot to bare foot. The English summer weather was true to form. "You see, I need to get back to my car to re-group. Time's getting on."

"We were alerted to attend a bomb," the officer said. "You are very fortunate that your car was not disposed of straightaway. Central London is on stand-by because of this incident. You've caused a lot of concern. You can't park here. Nobody can park here. You've actually driven through a police coned-off zone. Did you not feel their impact when you drove through them?"

"My mind has more to work on than traffic cones, officer! My mental dossier is weighty indeed. It involves you-know-who."

Jean tilted her thumb towards the Palace. The officer stifled a smile whilst Jean put him in the picture. "You are much mistaken, officer. I have diplomatic business. My credentials hail from a higher echelon than the Met. The Queen has summoned me and it is time I saw the Defender of the Faith."

"You don't want to be doing that. Not tonight, Madam. We're taking you to the station."

Jean considered his words. This was a scene change upon the stage of the world's theatre. Jean readily complied, half-listening for the applause of the bystanders, though she knew that her audience in heaven was sufficient. The leather gauntlet had also worked its magic; leather on men mingled with traffic fumes and hunger made an evening in a London prison most welcome. The company of these decent, leather-clad men was very acceptable indeed.

"I see," Jean said, a little playful. The officer looked at her and began to propel her forward. Jean decided that he was all man. A welcome diversion.

Curtain up on act two would be tomorrow. Jean pinched herself, aware that she was reeling and tripping on cue through a cinematic spectacle. Yes, she was awake and soon she would become a major cog in the world's most famous wheel – the Firm.

As she walked towards the police Maria she was sure a TV camera followed her progress. There was no red carpet, but it did occur to her that they might make a film of her life at a later date – perhaps a musical, even. She walked in stately, measured steps, imagining the newsreels and the adoring eyes of the world and the doubters. It was clear that she had nothing to hit but the heights.

"Everything's coming up roses!" Jean called towards the marksmen and police officers in attendance in a told-you-so sort of way.

* * *

"Did you eat it all Jean?" the officer asked.

"Yes. Thank you. Is my car ready?"

"You can't beat beans and chips, can you?" the officers at Charing Cross were very friendly. Part of their training, Jean thought. They were very skilled, and no one had blown her cover either. Another plus point.

"Yes. Anyway, I must be getting on. You know, things to do, *certain* people to see." Jean touched her nose knowingly. She was feeling much better with renewed energy. She had an overwhelming urge to dance, do the long jump, man a sea craft, wow the crowd on Centre Court – she felt utterly invincible. The prison surrounding did not deflate her mood. She'd taken to the cell like a duck to water. It was all meant to be.

"We just need to make sure all is well, Jean. We're going to take you to a hospital in London, the Gordon. It may be good for you to speak with a psychiatrist."

"Here in London? What about my dog?

"He's safe. Don't worry. You can pick him up soon."

Jean thought and then accepted the invitation. She was in the mood for sharing. There were so many important thoughts – nay, world-changing thoughts. It would be good to share the HRH dossier with a man of letters. Psychiatrists were educated and some had insight, thank goodness. She also wanted to test her skills and endurance to the limit, but more than that. It occurred to her that there was probably a 'plant' on the psychiatric ward, and it would be her duty to get them on board. She hadn't exactly been given a password, but she had noticed that she had been repeating phrases. 'That's the way the mop flops' being one in point.

"Okay, understood," Jean said leaning forward and making steely eye contact with the officer. "When are we going?"

"As soon as we can find you some shoes."

"A small detail," Jean said with a hand flourish.

* * *

"How are you feeling now, Jean? Come and join me to talk for a few minutes."

Jean was mid-stroke, her bat held horizontal to her chest. The ward had installed two table tennis tables in a bid to help the patients to not get fat. Fresh-faced, Jean bore down and took the shot, legs wide bent at the knee. The ping-pong ball landed on the corner of the table just on the line.

"That was in!" Jean shouted, panting and utterly exuberant. She swung round ready for the return. She pocked the ball again, higher this time and did a twirl, bat held aloft above her head, whirling Dervish fashion, returning to her position at the foot of the table tennis table. She crouched ready for the next shot and took it with show-stopping verve. She did a three hundred and sixty degree turn and then faced the psychiatrist.

"Tickadey-boo! Tickedy-boo!" Jean shouted. Her voice was quite high-pitched and clipped, but no matter. She looked at the man in front of her. He was of course educated and right up Jean's street. She knew instinctively that he would appreciate her piano playing, especially as he had just witnessed her world class ping-pong. She was a naturally talented, self-taught pianist and at one with the classical maestros. One day there would be an opening for her at the Albert Hall, but time enough for that. There were so many alternatives, opportunities. Every day on the ward Jean discovered just how incredibly gifted she was. Her aura said it all.

"And how are your thoughts at the moment?" the psychiatrist asked, raising his voice above the din on the ward. He had a bit of a hunted look about him, but that was to be expected. He was obviously not English, but Jean was broad-minded.

Beds were scarce. This was London and cosmopolitan; the home of the bizarre, the eccentric and the just plain mad. The chances were that his professional judgment would be that that Jean was well enough, and her leaving could make space for the next acute admission.

"How am I? Good. I'm good," Jean said laying down her paddle. She was still very animated and in full make-up.

"Let's have a few minutes in my office. We need to see if you can go home. Come in. Sit down."

Jean sat and looked at her psychiatrist. She was totally poised. "Yes," she said. "Ask away, ask away. There's so much to talk about."

"Jean, we have to assess whether it would be appropriate for you to return home to the Midlands. Do you feel your time here has helped?"

Jean took a deep breath and launched. "I've had the most bloody marvellous time. My aura has never been so fantastically vibrant. I never thought life could be so interesting in Pimlico. It's utterly splendid and I've made friends for life here. There's my little Juanito Sanchez-Morengo for a start. He's utterly tops. His father is a Brazilian coffee magnate more my age, very interested in the British monarchy and we have 'Jay-thus' in common, of course."

Jean rolled a Spanish 'th'. "That's the Son of God for the C of E amongst us. Yes. Do you want to know more? I suppose you do. I've had many a grand tête-à-tête with Lord Snooty. That's my name for him. He's tweeded up to the nines. I'm surprised he agreed to take off his gum boots. Little tinker! We have a great deal in common. Let me see. I like a shoot. I like the company of those who know how to knock up a gin and tonic. Bombay, you understand. I like my dogs. Always had them, even when overseas. I'm a patron of the RSPCA, you know, and…"

"Okay Jean," the psychiatrist interrupted Jean's reverie. He was satisfied that Jean was not a danger to herself or others. Tick. He had another twelve patients to assess that day. Jean had not presented a fixation with the British monarchy. Tick. She had not said she was the Queen. Tick. She had not said she was Jesus Christ or God. Tick. Clean bill of mental health. "How do feel about going home in the morning? Admin will supply a train ticket. Can someone accompany you? Your husband, perhaps?"

"No, not my husband. No. Not on any account… but there is someone. My dear Rolly. He works at Guys you know. I've been thinking about him a lot. A lot. He and I have a special connection. He – he stimulates me. He actually intrigues me, truth be told. Rolly is very good for me. He answers my needs. He knows how to do things. He's a natural. He is a man of the world, you know. Much travelled."

"Good, so your friend can accompany you."

"Oh yes." Jean was already imagining her travelling outfit. St. Pancras had such character. She and Rolly would take it by storm. "How bloody marvellous," Jean smiled, her aura never brighter.

* * *

"Pam? Hello Pam? Are you there?" Jean gripped her mobile phone, elbow extended.

"Hello. Is it Jean? Are you okay? Where have you been?"

"Pam, I'm back from London, but there's something else. I'm in a bit of a spot."

"Back from London?"

"Yes. I went back. You know, after the caravan and Hampton Court and the Concorde. It was the Queen, Pam. I had to see her. The police didn't blow my car up though. Anyway, Pam I've had the most bloody marvellous time. I've mixed with London's A-Listers at The Gordon Hospital. Very cultured. Pam, I've something to tell you. I've rekindled things with Rolly."

"Jean, calm down." Pam was trying to be firm.

"I have Pam. He met me from Guys. We caught a Virgin train. We had smoked salmon at St. Pancras and we didn't have to pay. He's a man who can make it happen. It was glorious Pam, and we had a G and T – spot on it was. My flame's re-ignited!"

Pam took a deep breath. "Okay, but you must stay calm Jean. Have you taken your tablets?" There was no answer. "Jean, where's Peter?"

"Gone, gone – he's history this time. The dog is fine; Robbie, my dear son, saw to him in Battersea. He's fine. More importantly, the Queen is fine. I'm fine…"

"Jean? Jean…?" Pam listened to the burring sound, the telephone line now dead. She wondered where Jean would go. Would she try to marry Rolly? Where was Peter? Hopefully, somebody would have some answers. She put down the phone and waited for the next call. The next of many.

6 Shades Within a Mirage

"You're going to have to do something, Pam," Ria stated categorically.

Pam drew deeply on her cigarette, shell-shocked. Jean had left the hotel in a flurry of chiffon and jewellery and enthralling expectation. It had all been so exhausting. Pam stifled a yawn and sat down in Ria's hotel room which was soon to become hers as well. The nights had been long and eventful, especially sharing a room with Jean – not the restful holiday she had imagined.

"The thing is Ria, I know Jean. You have to be careful. I don't want to do anything that could whip her up into a worse state than she is already. She may settle down if we keep calm. I hope so. I don't think I can stand another sleepless night. She's talked about every topic and so fast.

Never stopping. She's so excited. Everything's perfect. Let's hope she runs out of steam soon." Pam did not sound convinced.

"Rubbish. It couldn't get any worse," Ria stated in clipped English. "Call the police. Her children need to know that she's missing, last seen with an Arab."

"Well, she's not technically missing. She's – well, she's on a date. Oh, and he's not an Arab; he's a Tunisian."

"What bloody rubbish. I don't care what he is. She's alone with a foreigner who drives donkeys for a living. Pam, you know she's gone as high as a helicopter!"

"You mean kite."

"This is no time to correct my bloody English idioms. Do something! She needs treatment – a tablet or injection or something."

"And he drives camels for a living. He does have a donkey though, for his own use, I think."

"I'm not interested in the bloody detail. This is a crisis!"

"But she seemed happy enough when she left. Mind you, she had been on the wine most of the day. Anyway, I think she likes Ahmed because he reminds her of Omar Sharif when he was Lawrence of Arabia on horseback."

"It's a bloody donkey for God's sake!" Ria shouted, exasperated. She positioned herself near the hotel window, pushed back her hair with deliberation, stubbed out the tip of her cigarette and lit another with almost confident precision. She took a long draw on it and then faced Pam square on. "Pam, it has to be you who calls the doctor. It can't be me. The last thing I want is for her to say that the bloody German put her in the mental hospital. She'd make me suffer for it and go on suffering – and she'd throw me down the stairs."

"Well she did go willingly with Ahmed, Ria. She liked the way he treated the camels when she had a ride. You know that we can't tell Jean what to do. She's her own person."

"She's ill! Even though she doesn't think she is. That's part of the illness. They have no insight. She never takes her bloody tablets. Pam, you have to notify a doctor. If I did it, Jean would push me down the stairs. I know the look she gives me when she needs a sedative or something. We could all bloody die in our beds if she goes higher and higher."

"Give it another hour and we'll tell the holiday rep if she's not back by then. Anyway, I think I'll catch forty winks while I can. I need to. I hope Jean won't be offended when she realises I'm not sharing with her any more. But she's hardly slept at all and neither have I. I feel like a zombie."

Ria grimaced and raised her eyes to heaven. "Yes, get some sleep while you can. She won't even notice where you're sleeping."

Ria had said her bit. She was tired of talking, suggesting, persuading, dreading the next string of events. She knew it was going to be a long and sultry night. She looked out from the hotel window hoping to be distracted. The moonlight cast shadows into places she did not expect. Somewhere, hidden in the distance, she heard the faint barking of dogs. She half-expected Jean to appear, ghostly in her white, flowing kaftan, but thankfully she didn't emerge from the darkness. Where was she now? This was no joke.

She stared into the distance. It was a balmy evening full of muted sounds and movement. A firefly gave a pin hole of light to the night sky. She watched it turning in circles, flicking beads of light like diamond dust here and there. You must relax and be philosophical, she told herself. That's what her mother would have said. She sat back and nestled into the heat of the night and inhaled deeply on her cigarette. She relished the peace, no matter how short-lived. She stayed still in the darkness. She heard waiters talking lowly in foreign, sing-song voices below her room. She felt that their lives were simple, but happy enough. They had their lot in life and knew what tomorrow would bring. Oh that she did too.

Pam was now sleeping soundly.

* * *

The Tunisian sea breeze was sent by the Almighty. It soothed Jean and added to the moment as she journeyed with her new lover. She bathed in the breeze imagining it to be the breath of God himself. She lifted her face and shoulders to feel its cooling in the night. She adjusted her linen scarf and leafy head-dress, which she had crafted in a whimsical moment. She repositioned it with a stylish wrist action not dissimilar to that of Isadora Duncan, but far more poetic. She knew she cut a fine figure swathed in this particular outfit which showed the shape of her woman's body – its mystery, as yet, unrevealed to Ahmed.

Jean closed her eyes and gloried in her readiness. Soon she would feel his manly weight upon her. It would be perfect. She had taken life by its throat and held it hostage so that every sinew of who she was pulsed with life.

The moon hung above them, a clear white orb watching them. They journeyed forward. Jean closed her eyes and lost herself in the moment. The steady rhythm of the donkey's hooves pounded on and on between stone, sand and sun-hardened mud. Every so often, she swayed to the left then right with the contour of the terrain, her soul dancing in tandem. The not knowing where she was going adding extra exhilaration. She swallowed deep and hard, excited by every twist and turn. Her journey was punctuated by the sound of Ahmed's voice, dusky and beguiling under the cloak of the Tunisian night. Soon she would taste the desert sand in her mouth, his man's smell and her Fate.

"We come to my house Madame Jean." Ahmed's English was broken and enticing. The big event was near. She would be ravished and ravished again on the bed of a swarthy man. Bliss.

Jean shot Ahmed a shy, knowing glance enjoying the sight of him. He was a man, *her* man desiring *her*, his profile lighted by the broken fire flames from oil lamps snaked between the sand dunes. She saw him virile, bearded and sweating like a man does. She could not stop her hand rubbing his face, open-palmed, as he steered the donkey and cart towards where his bed lay, waiting for both of them. Jean threw back her head and yelped with abandoned joy. "Quickly!" she shouted.

Jean Riley

She held the moment. It consumed her like the kick of a good, stiff gin. She was living the Destiny hollowed out for her alone by the very hand of God. And there was more to come.

Tonight, Jean had it on the Highest Authority that she was to experience the mother of all orgasms. It was all in His Plan.

* * *

Within minutes, the rutted cart track gave way to a narrower passage. Heat hung in the crevices between squat, wooden buildings lighted by the ever present moon.

"We here now, lady. I take the care of you sexy, white lady with the gold in her eye. You gold in my heart Madame Jean," Ahmed said, eyeing the gold on Jean's wrists. "I give the good time. Yes, Madame?"

Jean sped into overdrive with thoughts and musings and words, and more words spilling from her. "Yes, soon, soon. Is this the way? Show me your room. Do you have something for us to drink? Let's see. Show me the best way in. Oh, and don't forget to give the donkey water. I've heard that some of you don't treat you animals well. So hurry up. Show me the way. Are we going to be alone? There is just you, isn't there? What do I call you?"

Ahmed halted his mule and held out his hand to hoist her from the donkey cart. They joined hands and her body tilted forward so that she was in his arms being lowered from the donkey cart into the passage way. Breathless, not noticing the smell of camel on her lover, Jean started to murmur what turned into an energetic rendition of Holst's The Planets Suite. Her humming became mesmeric and loud. She began to dance a bit. The searing, beating rhythm of the music in her head, the perfumed night, after-shock of red wine and the tightening hold of this dark, swarthy man was life itself.

Sacred paintings came into her mind's eye, rushing and mingling together. She was the Virgin Mary alighting the donkey in the 'Flight into Egypt', thrust forward into her Promised Land. Jean felt herself alive and utterly joyous in her understanding of the Lord's plan. It was all working out so magnificently, piece by piece fitting together wonderfully well and effortlessly. She decided at that moment that living in technicolour was her calling. It would be ridiculous to consider returning to the bland, plod of suburban life with the dull, dull people she had endured. Their greyness bored her. Their tiny horizons irritated her.

Ahmed did neither. He rubbed himself against the backs of her thighs, still trembling from the brunt of her journey by cart. He squeezed both her buttocks and set her vagina on fire. It leapt forward, eager and moist – further confirmation that she must go where the Spirit leadeth.

* * *

Once inside Ahmed's room, Jean's feverish expectation mingled with curiosity. She straddled the mattress, delighted in the intimacy of the obscured room. Sacking obliterated most of the window and closed them off from the night, though the moonlight peeped in at them through the cracks. Now anything could happen. Jean wriggled deliciously, making coquettish eye contact with Ahmed.

"Wine, Madame Jean. You want?" He approached the mattress with a full jam jar. Jean reached out and put the goblet to her lips. She drank its contents and used her tongue to coat her lips with what she believed to be fine Tunisian wine. Bacchus was alive again, imbibing with her.

"More!" she said forcefully, thrusting the jam jar back at Ahmed. "Do you know how to treat a real woman? More now. The best the best, and have some for yourself. I'm not here to be disappointed. A real woman knows what she wants. I hope you can satisfy me. That is what I am used to and that is what I will get. Quickly!"

Ahmed smiled good-naturedly. Jean did not see his rotten teeth. "Yes, I make you happy now."

At that he deposited the jam jar on a box which served as a table, threw back his head and began to wail. He pulled off his head dress then clutched his groin with theatrical fervour. Jean reached out and ruffled his pantaloons, grabbing his manhood with pleasurable force. As if on cue, Ahmed took a step backwards and made a whinnying noise not dissimilar to that made by his donkey, and then inserted his hand round about his cod piece. Jean watched wide-eyed and ready.

In due course, the pantaloon snake appeared, magnificently enhanced for Jean by the effects of wine. Ahmed, keen to make the most of what God had given him, began to hold himself aloft tilting himself at various angles at Jean's eye level. The situation looked more than promising from Jean's point of view. She noted that Ahmed lacked neither length nor girth, the former being enhanced significantly by Ahmed's ever quickening hand movements.

"You like?" he said swinging his member like a pendulum. With measured gusto Jean began to take part, cupping all that was red and throbbing, propelling Ahmed into a pleasing position on top of her. The heat began to rise, swirling within Jean's very own flights of fancy. The walls shimmered with images from the Arabian Nights as the lovers yo-yoed into each other amidst glorious ecstasy and grunting. There were camels loping, tent canvasses flapping, God's creatures squawking and feeding on carrion. Peter O'Toole was there too in Jean's thinking, dewy-eyed wearing his Sheik's head dress. For Jean, at that moment, Ahmed became Lawrence of Arabia. He smelt of desert, he was an officer and a gentleman and his warmth and wetness were electrifying – and ongoing until both were spent.

* * *

The moon was waning a little. The hotel balconies were all in darkness bar one. "Coo-ee, coo-ee Pam! Pam! Are you there?" Jean was back and all aglow.

Ria roused herself from her waking dream. She looked through the window to see Jean silhouetted against the skyline and the moon. She was leaning sideways from the neighbouring balcony facing towards Ria's room where Pam lay sleeping.

"Pam, where have you gone? I've had the most, bloody marvellous time. A good wine and a good man – what more could any woman ask for? Pam, answer me! Ria, don't be getting up to your tricks. Where's Pam?"

Ria took a deep breath and put on her glasses. She looked over to Pam still asleep in the dimmed light. She gathered herself together, leaned across and gave Pam a gentle nudge. She spoke in a low, clandestine voice, half asleep. "Pam, Pam, she's back. She's alive. Pam, wake up."

Pam stirred in the darkness, wondering where she was and what time of day or night it might be. Ria began to move towards the table where she'd left her cigarettes. She heard Jean's voice slip into a rhetorical address. "True passion isn't for the faint-hearted. Just like mercy, its quality cannot be strained. I have been to the mercy seat and back. Mercy, love, life droppeth from the night and from the hand of God. With God all things are possible. He holds me in the palm of his hand and tonight his plan worked a treat. All we have to do is put ourselves into the will of God. Tomorrow and tomorrow and tomorrow… the dawn walks over the shoulders of the night."

Jean needed the attention of her companions. Tonight was special, after all. She wanted to share it.

"Bloody wake up for God's sake. We're alive, alive-o… life is for living! This isn't a rehearsal, you know. For God's sake stir yourself. It's early yet! You're a long time dead, you know! Can you hear me Pam? Is Ria in there with you? Has she been at the Liebfraumilch? Any left?"

Pam began to gain consciousness. "Ria? Sounds like she's back."

"Yes."

"Where is she?"

"Hovering on the balcony like a bloody apparition waking the hotel."

"Thank God she's back and alive. How long has she been there?"

"I don't know," Ria said, resigned to what lay ahead. "You'd better have a cigarette before we go to investigate."

"Sounds like a good idea. Here we go again."

7   A Shade of Blood Red

"Jean, are you coming down for breakfast?" Pam knocked on Jean's door again, but there was still no answer. "Jean, is everything okay?"

Jean's eyes opened. "Yes, yes. I'm sleeping in today. See you at the beach later, Pam."

"Okay, see you later."

Pam set off towards the hotel dining room. She knew Ria was already there as she liked her early morning walk and cigarette, and her towel on the sunbed.

Jean looked out over the landscape across her balcony. She came into consciousness slowly. Too much vino had been drunk the night before and she was only sleeping a couple of hours each night. There was so much living to squeeze into this holiday. Time was racing by and so were Jean's thoughts.

The Tunisian sun rose like a red fist in the sky. Jean could see it punching through the crack in the curtains, red and strident. She stirred to look directly at it, though she knew this was unwise. Like a faithful friend, it was always there no matter where she had chanced to wake up during her holiday. Bar, room, beach, pool, settee, floor or saddle – there it was.

This morning, she rolled forward and sat herself upright on the settee in her room which had served as her bed for the last four hours or so. The night before, she had ridden the sand dunes of Heaven with Ahmed. Sleep had possessed her finally round about 3 am. She ached from the jostling of the night before, and as she moved her torso, she determined she was not to be camel or donkey cart riding again for the foreseeable future.

Jean looked down. There were traces of sand on the floor, but no knickers in sight. They must be somewhere. On her way to her en-suite she saw her panda eyes and bed hair framed in her hotel room mirror. She had that red-bronzed look as well, sun-kissed to a turn. She cut a distinguished sight and would have made a fine cameo on Tunisian coinage, she thought. Indeed last night she'd been the queen of Djerba as far as Ahmed was concerned. With him in mind and moistened tongue, Jean wet her finger and drew a figure 'one' in the air like men did when they notched up sex on the bedpost.

She was on holiday after all, and turning a head or two was to be expected. "Bloody marvellous! I regret nothing," Jean said aloud to herself, quite flushed in her second youth, a tad itchy below.

She padded to the bathroom and back, side-stepping at intervals imagining herself a temple dancer performing in front of smooth-thighed, cross-legged men, helpless in their admiration of her swaying abdomen and full, roughed lips.

Today Jean decided she would have some entertainment. Pam and Ria would be going to the beach to lay and sleep, and of course Ria would be reading her 'Spiegel' as usual. The pair of them seemed to need so much sleep. Jean could not understand why. Sleep was by no means sacred when there was living to be done with sallow complexioned men. Jean thought sagely to herself, 'we either do, or die'. She plumped for doing.

Do, she must, but what?

If in doubt or at a loose end, there was always champagne. That was the answer. The great thing was that it would materialise with a man bearing it. Just the ticket. Usually it was a dark man wearing a white shirt and trim, black trousers. Jean imagined the waiter's entrance to her room. He would arch down in front of her as he lowered the tray and she would see the shape of his buttocks. There she could judge whether they were her cup of tea or not. He would have to be dashing and smell like a man.

Waiters waited. That was the good thing about having them on tap. It was like the unwritten rule of the jungle – or desert in this case. Jean's wish would be his command. And Jean was in a commanding mood. Last night she had unleashed her dominatrix good and proper. The warmth and heft of a lithe man doing her bidding was not to be sneezed at. What was there not to like?

Time was of the essence. None of us were getting any younger – and with that thought Jean rang for Room Service.

* * *

He entered tall and smartly cool, his eyes darkly softened by laughter lines. He was a beautiful man, and he was in her room and of course, he was, Jean assumed, eager to please. But she would have sport first.

"Put the tray here," Jean said, irritated because she wanted no barrier between herself and the body of this big, dark man. She noticed his hair was smooth and fulsome. She wanted to eat it. She imagined pulling it in sex-play and pushing it behind his ears, baring his classic bone structure which she would lick and bite as the mood took her until she made him bleed, or he master her. She giggled at the thought of the latter.

Jean sat still, her neck tilted back then forward as she examined his waiting, Tunisian body. His shoulders were wide, leading to arms strong enough to throw her up into the firmament and catch her again coming down. Holst's Planets were already refraining in the background. Jean could feel them sighing in her inner ear.

"Pour now!" Jean commanded nodding towards the champagne. "And one for you too."

"Yes, of course."

His English was crisp with just enough of the foreign about it. Jean imagined him as a foreign correspondent working for the BBC. She liked the idea of native made good. And she had it in her to give him a break if he pleased her well enough.

His hands were graceful and strong. She saw them next to the white cloth which wrapped the champagne bottle. Every part of him excited her.

"Sit here and drink," Jean said patting the settee and slugging her champagne. "Shirt off. Remove," she commanded at her waiter, flicking her fingers in the air in charades mode showing him what she wanted him to do. "Nobody will see you. The blinds are down, and my friends next door are asleep. We're safe."

"One moment, Madame. There is more for you from our kitchen. They send it." He moved back towards the hotel room door and soon appeared next to Jean with yet another tray. "The smoked salmon and flat bread for you. They send it. It is good." He held the tray for her approval.

Not the slightest bit hungry, Jean looked up ready to dismiss what the kitchen had prepared, but she stopped herself when she set her eyes on to the corner of the tray beyond the food. She stared, her eyes softening their gaze. There, slightly leaning, rested one perfectly formed, blood-red rose.

"For you, Madame," the waiter said, holding the crimson token forward for Jean to take.

She reached out, both arms fully extended with flattened palms. She picked up the rose, fragrant red, and flailed it with feather lightness across her face with her right hand. She extended her tongue to feel the petals' silk across her lips. Her mouth was fully open, plump and pink red. She ran the stem and thorn tips across her tongue and lips, playing with each thorn with the soft of her tongue biting and sucking until she reached the head of the rose again full in her mouth.

She opened her eyes wide now and held the rose in front of her. She imagined she was the heroine enduring the opera's final scene where hopeless love and death mingled in one breathless climax. She lay down, her ruby-coloured kaftan up high around her waist, her buttocks slithering against the settee's velour. Her waiter was attentive and took position. The rose rocked this way, then that, in unison with her buttocks. Likewise, her knees flexed shiny, pointing to heaven as she yo-yoed up and down.

"Again!" Jean shouted, and still Holst's The Planets held its sway, pounding in her ears. Music was the food of love, after all. Jean lost herself in the rhythmic rise and fall.

She half-lived the opera's climax now in her mind's eye, plucking at the waiter's shirt buttons and chest hair with frenetic gusto. So much so that he lost his footing and fell across Jean's thighs, the rose now lodged in her bosom above his head. He held on to the settee base trying to right himself in order to restore normality. Not quite understanding the role he must play, he had the presence of mind to draw breath whenever the opportunity presented itself. Ever valiant, he was unaccustomed to a flesh fest on this scale.

Jean did not notice that his eyes were beginning to water.

In full flight, Jean clutched at the rose again, lathering her flesh red with dislodged petals. The opera dame in her wondered did her mouth bleed now? She imagined the blood red tide smearing her flesh. She hoped her lips had pressed the last thorn hard enough to draw blood. She fancied herself up there with the finest operatic heroines experiencing love and the bleed of lung TB simultaneously. TB was rife in those days, as was real passion, Jean mused. She remembered Nicole Kidman in 'Moulin Rouge' magnificent in a blood-rich tragedy, commanding centre stage with passion. Her waiter waited. She would have him again.

Spurred on, Jean wrapped her fist in her his shirt in a great knot, and began to tug at it with the vigour of a woman who would be satisfied.

"Get 'em off!" Jean shouted even louder pulling at her waiter's manhood, which had awakened inside his pulled-apart hipsters. "All off, now!"

Accordingly, he obeyed as quickly as he was bid. He shimmied his trousers all the way down to his ankles whilst still horizontal, sliding and bouncing dutifully into Jean again for all he was worth.

"Bravo, bravo!" Jean yelled, thumping hard with her fist wherever it landed.

* * *

"Jean, Jean! Are you awake?"

A voice outside killed the moment. Jean rolled sideways away and cocked her ear. It was Pam's unmistakeable voice. Jean untangled her left leg and dislodged her waiter's right leg which was half kneeling, half standing. Jean motioned for him to move out of the way, pushing her hand over his mouth as she did so, making sure that he was incapable of speech. No one must know that she had bedded a waiter. Jean was in no mood to explain or justify. She knew Pam and Ria would, of course, give her grief about AIDS.

"Jean, we're going for a bit of a walk round the garden. We'll see you down there!" Pam shouted.

Jean worked her way on to her feet and moved so that she was able to talk to Pam from a crouched position through the closed door. "Yes, okay. See you in a bit," Jean called in her normal voice, not wanting to give the game away.

She turned to look for her waiter. Within seconds he had made himself look respectable. He stood by the tray and the cloth holding the Champagne bottle poised to pour Jean's second glass.

"Would you like another glass now, Madame?" he asked with averted eyes smothering a nervous cough.

"Go!"

"Madame, I…"

"Go," Jean said with an imperious wrist action loosening her watch and proffering it. "Just go."

Go, he did, and swiftly too.

* * *

Today was home time. Time to pack.

Jean was determined to travel in what had become her favourite kaftan. She would taxi in it to the airport, hoping her companions would not close in forcing her to change and think about arrival in cold English weather. Jean did not wish to be sensible. She would wear it on the aircraft plush like a foreign dignitary. And there was her pièce de résistance – her fez, scarlet red and placed at a jaunty angle. Unmissable. Perfect.

She took a moment. She regarded herself in her hotel room mirror from every angle, mimicking a royal wave. She adjusted her posture so that the arcs of her derriere and calf muscle were accentuated and set nicely to mirror the angle of her fez. She liked the cut of her jib. Her encounters with the Tunisian male this past fortnight had proved that she'd still 'got it'; it being the ability to drive men wild with desire.

There was a tap on her door. "Jean! Jean, are you there? Taxi coming in five minutes. Are you ready?" It was Pam again checking that she was on target time-wise. They must get her to the airport.

"Yes. See you in the lobby," Jean answered, thinking on the spot, deflected from her thoughts.

The holiday had been too good to be true in some ways, and yet there was something stirring in the bowels of Jean's soul, something ruddy and sore. She had been chosen this fortnight, her womanhood redefined. She felt an overwhelming at-oneness with women of the world and those ones found described in quality fiction; women who had lived and had their rebirth in mid-life.

Jean dwelt on her epiphany. Something portentous took a hold of her – like the coming of the plague or fire scorching the red firmament, or wild dogs growling with bloody jowls, and graves opening for the dead to rise aloft into rosy glory. Images and the sounds of the nether world filled Jean's senses with no warning. Caesar's wife had had the very same second sight the night before the bloody dagger did away her husband. Jean knew she was in the company of great women. Without warning, she assumed the consciousness of Mrs. Morel in 'Sons and Lovers', heady and reeling with the scent of dew-damp flowers in the space-time continuum of her womanhood.

To hell with the packing. The taxi could wait. Jean was a new woman. She had been re-born this holiday through trial, error and sheer, cataclysmic orgasm with the men of the East. A holiday of a lifetime, no less.

Moved beyond herself, Jean picked up what remained of the red rose delivered by her waiter the night before. She fancied that an anchor in time was essential, a reference point for her biographers. She must leave her signature. She placed the rose on to the bed cover partly hiding the stem in the creases she had fashioned. With a steady hand, bordering on the theatrical, Jean dribbled the dregs from a red wine bottle she had discarded earlier on in the week. She looked at the tableau she had created of rose, part damaged and wine soaked, looking like blood. It pleased her – the blood, the rose. Her virginity lost, her womanhood re-born. She smiled to herself, and pitied other women who could never hope to be the sexualised creature she had become anew in mid-life. She eyed the motif she had created again. Here was real body – her life-blood pictured and caught in time. She imagined the reaction of the woman who would see it when she came to clean the room. How they would envy

Jean. Other women would too, Jean thought with some satisfaction.

She thought of those others. Always. It was the least she could do. She considered what might be a suitable grand gesture. A way of including other women to provide them with a hope of rejuvenation. Jean was all for sharing.

Then it came to her – once she got home she must remember to do her entry online for Trip Advisor so that other women could have a taste of what she'd had. The sun, the men, the wine. She remembered them all now as her tongue played with the thorn's pin prick from when she had bitten her waiter's rose.

Humanity... a suitable case for treatment!

I hope the narratives you've read, or will read, in this collection have raised a smile or two, and maybe they have led you to consider certain questions. The narratives are frank and funny largely because Jean wanted them to be entertaining. When Jean asked me to put her verbal snippets into narrative form, she was very clear that she must not be portrayed as a victim of any 'condition', bi-polar, mania – call it what you will. Undoubtedly, psychiatric conditions can have a serious impact on those who suffer. However, Jean speaks of being at her most creative when in bi-polar episode or mania. She positively enjoys this aspect of her 'self', even though she says that once the 'episode' is behind her, she has felt a bit foolish at times! She speaks of the danger involved in giving oneself over to the condition.

None of the narratives intend to encourage anyone to take part in unsafe fancies. The narratives are not intended to offend people or play down the seriousness of the condition. Medication has made significant improvements to the lives of some sufferers, and can be absolutely vital in winning back stability and good relationships. Neither are the narratives intended to offend anyone or belittle the power of a sincere, personal faith.

Bipolar is very much in the news today in our western popular press, and is even regarded as something to be sought out by celebrity, the wealthy or the bored. Truly though, some have bipolar 'thrust upon them'. We inherit the condition, and work to be free from it, or at least manage it so that it, and its medication, does not steal our lives. I admire those I know who have made a life with friendships, relationships, work and interest despite the loss and the trauma the condition has caused.

What About Those of Us Who Don't Have a Label?

Like me, I guess you can identify people in your life who show some of the *traits* which are now associated with this or another psychiatric condition. They probably don't have any diagnosis at all. We may live with eccentrics, the melancholy or someone who is just too full on. Perhaps you are one of these people. They walk amongst us!

The episodes recounted in Jean's life also throw up the *pathos* associated with our *human condition* in general, whether we have a 'label' or 'diagnosis' or not. We all share both destructive and life-giving behaviours at different times during the course of our lives. We don't generally *label* these behaviours, unless we rely on labels to give us some kind of identity for security, attention or use as an avoidance tactic – or maybe the labels are given to us by the health professionals because they have had cause to become involved.

The Pursuit of Extremes

It has always amazed me that some people I know well have a psychiatric diagnosis, and yet other people who display the *same* habits are *not diagnosed* with anything!

It is doubly amazing that some people actively *choose to generate the symptoms* associated with bi-polar to get a kick or a buzz. Isn't it commonplace for people to choose to 'get off their heads' with drink, particularly in our western culture? They fantasise for fun. Is this delusion? 'Escaping the hum-drum' is totally acceptable. We max out credit cards to spend, spend and spend. The irony is that the bi-polar sufferer is told **not** to carry out the behaviours which a high percentage of the population **do** carry out for fun – and to hell with the consequences!

The bi-polar sufferer is said to:
- get out of kilter
- talk a lot
- drink too much

- seek out sex
- spend too much money
- have extreme views
- do 'daredevil' things
- be very creative
- have obsessions
- love life and the grand gesture
- become easily irritated
- overstate their case
- give way to imaginings… flights of fancy
- get hyperactive and have racing thoughts, but grow bored a good deal of the time
- contradict themselves and others
- make decisions they may regret later
- be irrational and yet show great logic within their own framework of thought
- change their mind and judgements radically
- do U turns
- believe they are a person of note, title or superpower
- be both thoughtless and attentive
- be a trial to be with and are yet be the popular socialite

Have you recognised yourself yet? You're probably in there somewhere!

Those of us with no psychiatric labels may actively pursue all or some of the above at some point or other. Maybe we are more skilled at putting the brake on, thereby avoiding the need for drug therapy, and probably we don't have a family history of mental instability of any note. The elusive 'chemical imbalance' may not have caused a level of disquiet serious enough for intervention. There, but for the grace of God…

Seeing

Maybe you are looking to change the behaviour of those around you. Think again… are you open-minded enough to reflect on how your behaviour emerges, and how you're seen by others? Is there something about you that you'd love to change, adapt or exorcise? Would it be easier for others if you were a little more moderate?

Jean may have been diagnosed with bi-polar along with thousands of other people, including some of my closest friends. Good friends are regularly described as 'eccentric', have Asperger's, are bigoted, odd – call 'em what you will. I guess I am in there too! Weird, unconventional, awkward, shy, demanding, eccentric, longsuffering, bossy, esoteric, secretive, enigmatic… are you there too? If our at times 'strange ways' don't put us at risk, then most of us just live with the ups and downs.

Your Hand on the Rudder...

I hope the narratives open your mind to consider yourself or maybe a friend or family member. Wouldn't it be great to be able to have *insight* and shed some of the *troublesome habits* that stalk your life and relationships with others? It's possible. I testify to this. So, start with a quick, honest rundown of what makes you 'you'.

What *motivates* you, and what do you want your life to be like?

_____

Which people do you admire, and *why*?

_____

What behaviours have you *learned from childhood* and over the years?

_____

What would you like to *change*?

_____

How do you think your behaviour appears, and how do you think it *affects others*?

Can you see *patterns in your behaviour that you've adopted* in certain circumstances? Why?

Who do you love, care for, take joy in, judge, condemn, despise, get at or torment and why?

Why do you think your life contains strained or *broken relationships*?

Is anything ever your fault, and do you *regret* anything?

Do you feel you have to *pretend* to be happy in certain company?

___

Do you have a *public face and a private you*? How are they different?

___

What would really make you happy and *contented*?

___

What makes your mood low?

___

The Beast with Claws

Being human means we are, by default, vulnerable and that our 'human heart' can be 'desperately wicked' above all things. No wonder some of our species adopt the rules of the jungle to 'get them before they get us'! We possess the so-called reptilian brain for good or for bad. Maybe we need to start attempting to trim the claws of the beast within us. Rude, devious, self-seeking and self-obsessed behaviour is actually quite normal to encounter. Fruits are there too, fruits that nourish the beast and give life – love, peace, self-control, empathy, heroism.

We have cultivated our capacity to be guarded or like warriors, believing this to be our 21st century armour to shield us against 'the slings and arrows' of life tossed our way. We human beings are exposed to behaviours, and we learn them. We mimic the behaviours of others, good and bad, in our lives. We love and dread the behaviours of our children. We nurture useful, selfless and also brattish, gravely destructive behaviours in our kids and those around us. We live in our moods and the 'me' centric culture – the jewel in the crown of the West. We have made idols, not of stone, but of our own flesh and blood. How extreme these behaviours are seems to have a bearing on whether we are labelled by the health professionals or not. Some of us have our beasts named by them, some of us do not!

We're exposed to self-obsessed behaviour in *the media* day after day, often accompanied by desperate emotional need in those who are trying to be the image of success and the envy of all. We feel the brunt in the supermarket, on the road, and even in our own front rooms at times! I'm alright Jack, and the rest of you can lump it. I'm right and you lot are falling short. You're thick, fat, old, need a boob job, lack a man with a lucrative pension, and don't possess a designer handbag etc.… Poor me. Poor us. Poor them! Are we mentally ill or just normal? Is it society that has the personality disorder and are we the unsuspecting victims of the 'must-have' culture we live in?

Bucking the Trend

Wouldn't it be wonderful to live innocently in the Eden we have lost, be loved and loving and totally at one with each other and our Maker? Utopia – a place where we need not even think about behaviours to cultivate, shun or mimic. In one of Jean's remembrances, when separating from a husband, she speaks about attaining 'peace', and enjoying the sensation! We need conflict, and yet we say we want contentment. Such is the contradiction we are born to. In truth, there is something within us that tells us we can fall in love, nurture children, care for a lonely neighbour, care about commitment to work, give to those with little hope, and even die for causes we hold to be moral and just. Yes, we do still have these urges, but it's unfashionable to admit these things. There is almost an expectation that we must be cynical. We apply our own gags, and must not speak about the simple, decent things. It isn't cool. In fact you'd probably be laughed at or called a religious freak, a do-gooder or be locked up! Or, perhaps you'd be labelled bi-polar…

To dare to suggest that we can live a happy and contended life with modest finance, plain looks and few possessions would be regarded as insanity by most people in our western way of thinking today.

We're told we have to look perfect, be the best, want more, never be satisfied and attack anyone who stops us from getting what we want. We live in a world where the 'cult of self' rages in our faces, ears and sensibilities everyday of our lives. Our opinion is God. This is our post-modernist fate, whether we have a psychiatric label or not.

Indeed we are the children of the 'selfie'! We are bombarded by image, air-brushed or otherwise. The media tells us what we should look like, what we should aspire to, what we really must possess, and what we should deplore or destroy. The pursuit of all these things leads to 'extreme' behaviours, which some describe as bi-polar. Why do some people feel a need to copy-cat celebrities? Social media models behaviours for us, attacks us if we show any chink in the armour, any vulnerability or individuality. Society and the media tell us it's normal to be:

- selfish
- self-opinionated
- self-seeking
- self-conscious
- self-deluded
- self-destructive.

However, there are some individuals who can still manage to be:

- self-reliant
- self-effacing
- self-giving.

A Matter of Degree

It's no secret that human beings, with or without bipolar, are full of contradictions. Personal point of view can also distort our grasp on reality. Delusion, self or otherwise, is part of everyday life in one way or another. However, we can **consider** what we see, think and experience. This can actively enable us to make some helpful decisions to impact on your day, and your life with others.

Focus on people you know or yourself. The following can guide your considerations:

When does a confident person become a demanding or arrogant person?

_____

How do we decide when our own or another person's behaviour has '*crossed the line*'?

_____

Where do we define the '*tipping point*' to be in someone's personality, when we feel they've '*gone too far*'?

_____

Why is it okay for some people to behave in a certain way, but we judge the same behaviour to be unacceptable if another person does it?

Words and Identity

Have you noticed how we use various codes to describe people near to us? Usually these are friends or family members we care about – though at times they can be a 'trial' to be with. I guess you've heard people say things like 'he's a character, isn't he?' Sometimes we just refer to somebody as an 'individual' or a bloody nuisance!

We do hide behind words because we really don't want to be seen to be narrow-minded or judgemental. The words we use are often 'endearments' for the people we care about, but their traits can present challenges for even the most worldly-wise or tolerant amongst us.

Likewise, you may display these traits and never give them a second thought – until now! Behaviour habits become part and parcel of who we are. Being human as we are, bolstering our ego comes naturally. Consequently, whether you are bi-polar or not, *we positively revel in the very behaviours that other people dread to encounter in us!* It is difficult to look at our own behaviour traits and how these affect other people, but it is worth doing. *Name it and shame it, then control it!*

Most people want to improve their mood, their attitudes to life and enjoy good relationships.

Most people would rather *not* develop a condition which requires a psychiatric diagnosis, and the maze of treatments associated with that.

Root Out, Level or Axe

At times, do you feel the need to keep on *talking* and *don't* seem to need *sleep*?

Are there times when thoughts seem to be going *too fast in your mind*?

Do you have *obsessions*? Never? Regularly? All the time? How do these obsessions affect those around you?

Are there times you decide to do potentially *dangerous* things, or other people have told you that you do dangerous things too often? Describe what and when.

Do you make decisions to *binge on alcohol, loud music, drugs or sex* to stimulate or heighten your mood? How often?

_____

Has this habit led to self-harm, violent words or *behaviours targeted at others*? How many broken relationships are there in your life?

_____

Do you say platitudes? When and where do you *cause others* to be irritated, frightened or confused?

_____

When and where have you humiliated or caused anxiety for a *particular person or group* of people? Does this give you a 'high'?

_____

What *triggers* these behaviours you carry out?

_____

What kinds of *physical feelings* do you get when you speak or act out these behaviours?

_____

Describe the feelings, the *buzz or the high* you feel when your behaviour makes an impact on a particular person or group of people.

_____

Do you seek revenge against particular people at particular times? Describe these times.

_____

Describe a time you have experienced *regret*.

_____

Describe a time when you have managed to *forgive and forget*.

_____

When do you feel vulnerable?

_____

Levelling your See-Saw

At regular intervals, or when in the throes of a specific situation, some people find it helpful to carry out a form of self-scrutiny. This exercise can be a useful tool to decide what you need to do, or stop doing so much.

It may be useful for you to do this. Judge how your life is panning out. You are in charge. Use the questions above as a guide to identify the 'traits' it would be good to moderate or axe!

Extreme	Okay Me	Too Extreme

Enjoy the journey – whether you choose the middle passage or verge on extremes at times. Listen to trusted friends, and take your doctor's advice. Most importantly, stay safe and in control!